The Fryeburg Chronicles
Book VI

The Fryeburg Chronicles

The Life and Times of a Country Doctor

Book VI

June O'Donal

XULON PRESS

Xulon Press
555 Winderley Pl, Suite 225
Maitland, FL 32751
407.339.4217
www.xulonpress.com

Xulon PRESS

© 2024 by June O'Donal

All rights reserved solely by the author. The author guarantees all contents are original and do not infringe upon the legal rights of any other person or work. No part of this book may be reproduced in any form without the permission of the author.

Due to the changing nature of the Internet, if there are any web addresses, links, or URLs included in this manuscript, these may have been altered and may no longer be accessible. The views and opinions shared in this book belong solely to the author and do not necessarily reflect those of the publisher. The publisher therefore disclaims responsibility for the views or opinions expressed within the work.

Unless otherwise indicated, Scripture quotations taken from the King James Version (KJV)–*public domain.*

Paperback ISBN-13: 979-8-86850-249-1
Ebook ISBN-13: 979-8-86850-250-7

TABLE OF CONTENTS

Historical Fiction: What is Fact and What is Fiction?...... ix
The Miller Family Tree............................. xiii
Acknowledgements xv
Prologue..xvii
Map Of Fryeburg, Maine........................... ix

I Scarlett Fever 1
II Apoplexy 9
III A Busy Sunday..................................18
IV The Amputation 26
V Mr. Bennett.....................................33
VI Tetanus 46
VII Charlie's First Day Back in School................58
VIII Charlie's New School 70
IX The Accident 82
X Long Road to Recovery 93
XI Graduation....................................103
XII Vienna, Austria 115
XIII Warsaw, Poland..............................121
XIV Cousin Thaddeus 126
XV 1876 Centennial Exhibition 136
XVI Autumn of '76...............................150
XVII Hero of the Ice Harvest 155
XVIII The New Church 168

XIX Beginnings and Endings 177
XX Mr. Peary... 192
XXI Seeking.. 209
XXII Commitments 228
XXIII A Wedding and a Tragedy 237
XXIV New York 244
XXV Changes 251

Historical People..................................... 264
Fryeburg Landmarks 271
Discussion Questions................................. 279
The Fryeburg Chronicles: Own the Entire Series......... 281
End Notes 287
Bibliography 293

Historical Fiction: What is Fiction and What is History

The Miller family are fictional characters. James and Sarah Miller were one of the early homesteaders in Fryeburg, in the Province of Maine in the colony of Massachusetts. They had three sons, Ethan, Micah, and Benjamin. Ethan left Fryeburg as a young man and settled in Williamsburg, Virginia. Micah inherited the family farm; his three children eventually settled in Buffalo, New York. They play an integral role in the first three books in the series.

It is Benjamin Miller and his descendants who we will follow on our journey of *The Fryeburg Chronicles*.

The Chase, Anderson and Jackson families are fictional as well.

The history of Fryeburg is filled with Osgood, Walker, Bradley, Weston, and Evans families. If someone is mentioned by Mr. or Mrs. without their first name, they are fictional. If their full name is given, they are historical people and they will be listed at the conclusion of story.

River View Farm and Evans General Store are fictional locations. All other landmarks will also be listed with photographs at the conclusion.

The Fryeburg Chronicles Book VI

Whether you are a first-time reader, or a follower of the series, you may wish to review the Miller Family Tree.

Synopsis of Book V *After the Battle*

Jacob Miller's youngest son, Isaac, his best friend Darian Flynn, Jacob's grandson David and his best friend, Monroe Quint join the Union Forces during the War Between the States. Their lives are changed forever at the Battle of Gettysburg!

Monroe Quint, a historic person, is killed and buried at Gettysburg.

After Isaac is severely wounded in battle, Darian saves his life, when he leaves his post to carry him to a nearby farmhouse to receive medical treatment. He risks his own life to mail a letter to Fryeburg begging someone to come to Gettysburg with food, medicine, and clean bandages before Isaac dies of infection from his leg amputation. Unfortunately, as he is returning to his post, he is captured by the Confederates, and eventually sent to Andersonville Prison.

David Miller, confused and dazed, is missing in action for months. It is cousin, Thaddeus Pierce, a newspaper reporter who is in Gettysburg to report on the new national cemetery, who discovers a disoriented soldier hiding in the woods. When he realizes the young man is David Miller, who is obviously suffering from 'soldier's heart', Thaddeus escorts him back to Fryeburg to be reunited to his father, Eli, and family.

Isaac forges discharge papers so David will not be charged with desertion. After a traumatic incident, this troubled young man confesses to Isaac that he discovered a severely injured and abandoned Confederate soldier screaming in pain. He shot him to put him out of his misery and can no longer live with the guilt.

When David goes missing one night, Eli and Isaac find his body hanging from the rafters in the barn. They staged his body to make it look like he accidentally fell from the hayloft and broke his neck.

It is now Isaac who is tortured by family secrets!

Miller Family Tree

Benjamin Miller m. Hannah Chase Miller
b. 1769-d. 1853   b. 1760's-d. 1857

First Preceptor of Fryeburg Academy

Quaker Abolitionist

Attorney, Judge, U.S. Senator

Secretly a former light-skinned slave Abolitionist

Abolitionist

Teacher of freed blacks

Jacob Miller
b. 1794

Married Katherine Wiley in 1813

Farmer, owner of River View Farm Law Firm

Abigail Miller Pierce
b. 1796 d. 1857

Married Joshua Pierce in 1824

Assisted in Miller & Pierce

Thaddeus Pierce
b. 1825

Journalist/ World traveler

Elijah Miller	Daniel Miller	Rachel Miller	Isaac Miller
b. 1814	b. 1816	b. 1820	b. 1838
Married Julia Frye	Married Emily Walker	Married Peter Evans	Married Lydia Merrill
Farmer	Owned Lumber Mill	Worked in textile mill	Wounded in Gettysburg
Fair Trustee	Boarding house for Academy students	Businesswoman	Founded apothecary.
Becky Miller	Academy Students	Outspoken on	**Summer Miller**
b. 1838	No biological children	temperance and	b. 1857
Victoria Miller	Took in Irish orphan	women's right to	**Mahayla Miller**
b. 1840	**Darian Flyn**	vote	b. 1858
David Miller			**Charlie Miller**
1843-1864			b. 1867

Acknowledgments

I am neither an historian nor a scholar; I am a storyteller and an educator. My objective is to teach local, Maine and American history through the experiences of the fictional Miller family. History is the stories of ordinary (and occasionally extraordinary) people living their lives in a specific time and location. It is more than names and dates. It encompasses the inventions, architecture, occupations, literature, philosophies, religion, politics, moral and physical conflicts, fashion, food, science, medicine, inventions, and geography!

Writing is a solitary endeavor. Researching takes a village! I am indebted to the Fryeburg Historical Society for access to historical records and history books in their research library and their permission to reproduce historic photographs. Thank you, Linda Drew for finding numerous documents for me, and for sharing a family tragedy to her great-grandmother which inspired the chapter on the fictional Anderson family.

I would like to thank the Fryeburg Historical Society for allowing me to photograph the front cover in their museum, The Samuel Osgood House on 83 Portland Street in Fryeburg. The cover includes Dr. William Towle's desk, a vintage doctor's bag, an antique Bible, teapot, teacup, and two owls from Robert Peary's taxidermist business when he lived in Fryeburg

The Fryeburg Chronicles Book VI

from 1877-79. Also, my thanks to the Currier Doll Collection of Fryeburg, for use of the antique rag doll with a porcelain face.

Prologue

Humble farmer, Jacob Miller, the son of Senator Benjamin Miller is now the family patriarch and the owner of the family homestead, River View Farm, located by the Saco River. All four of his children now reside in Fryeburg in 1875.

Eli, the eldest son, and farmer lives just across from the river and has devoted his entire life working on the farm with his father. His son David was killed in an "accident", his daughter Victoria moved to Portland, while his daughter Becky remained in Fryeburg.

His second son, Daniel, a man of faith, sold his lumber mill after the war and built a large home next door to the farm. He and his wife, Emily, operate a busy boarding house for Fryeburg Academy students. Having no biological children, they took in an Irish orphan, and loved Darian as if he was their son. Tragically, he died as a prisoner of war in Andersonville Prison on the last day of the Civil War.

His ambitious and opinionated daughter, Rachel, is a member of the Temperance Society, believes women should have the right to vote, and is a very successful businesswoman. She and her husband, Peter Evans, have two sons who live out of state.

The youngest son, Isaac, is a generation younger than his siblings. He nearly died during the Battle of Gettysburg from an infection after a leg amputation. He greatly struggled upon his return home to adapt to his responsibilities as husband and father to young daughters, Summer, and Mahayla. His mother encouraged him to find a new career as an apothecary, after it became evident, he could no longer farm. Their son, Charlie, was born after the war while Isaac was attending medical school. The family returned to Fryeburg to establish his medical practice in his grandfather's large home.

FRYEBURG

Scale 1/4000

BUSINESS DIRECTORY

Dry Goods & Groceries
- Stroat & Higgins
- E. Weeks & Co
- T. C. Ward
- H. C. Buswell
- P. Eastman

Attorneys
- E. L. Osgood
- J. R. Bradley

Physicians
- F. B. Bradley
- I. Towle

Jeweller
- Jas. Lord

Shoe Maker
- W. Hall
- H. & O. Morton

Carpenters
- P. W. Swan
- R. Tinge
- A. Emerson

Tanners
- M. H. Allen
- H. M. Buswell

Harness Maker
- John Evans

Wheelwright
- J. C. Ward

I

Scarlet Fever

Fryeburg, Maine April 1875

"Mama! Charlie is dying!" seventeen-year-old Summer Miller screamed from her brother's second-floor bedroom. Her younger sister, Mahayla, sat silently on the small bed holding down her convulsing brother.

Lydia Miller glanced at the clock in her husband's office which read ten minutes past midnight. She held up her skirts in one hand, and ran up the front staircase leaving her desk, her ledger, and papers.

Lydia had become a fastidiously organized woman, efficiently running Isaac's Miller's medical practice, her household, and raising her three children. Shortly before his marriage in 1856, Isaac inherited his grandfather, Senator Benjamin Miller's large, furnished home on the corner of Main Street and Bridge Street.[1] The people of Fryeburg who remembered her as a young, inexperienced, and ill-prepared newlywed marveled at the dramatic transformation.

She had struggled raising her two daughters while her husband was fighting in the War Between the States. She could not cope when Isaac returned from Gettysburg, recuperating from a leg amputation. Unable to meet the rigors of farming, Isaac with his mother's and wife's assistance, began a successful apothecary business. This is when Isaac decided to become a doctor.

Upon completion of medical school at Bowdoin College in Brunswick, Maine in 1870 the family, which now included their son, Charlie, returned to their home, and Isaac converted his grandfather's law office into his medical offices. Lydia had quickly adapted to her new responsibilities. Their lives, though hectic, ran smoothly, until four months ago, when a scarlet fever epidemic broke out.

Isaac worked around the clock as he made house calls, treating children, and consoling parents. He returned home only to eat, sleep, and change his clothes. Initially Lydia was not overly concerned, for both their daughters had fully recovered from scarlet fever years ago and were now immune. Isaac had pulled Charlie out of school when one of his classmates died of the dreaded disease, hoping their son would be spared.

This bright, fun- loving, eight-year-old dutifully completed his schoolwork and chores in the mornings and assisted his mother with the office work in the afternoons and evenings. He excelled in math, and accurately recorded patients' payments be it cash, bartered produce, or services in the ledger.

Three months ago, Charlie complained of a sore throat, nausea, and exhaustion. The familiar red rash and swollen lymph nodes in his neck appeared. His temperature continued to rise, as his condition worsened. He had developed rheumatic fever, with joint pain, fatigue, headache, chest pains, and a dangerously high temperature.

Summer and Mahayla alternated in taking days out of Fryeburg Academy to care for Charlie, while Lydia ran the busy office.

Lydia was out of breath when she reached Charlie's room.

"Papa should be here!" Mahayla accused.

"He is with Mr. Parker, who is alone and dying," Lydia reminded.

"Old man Parker is a good-for-nothing drunk, who is drinking himself to an early grave. Papa should be here! Charlie is dying!"

Lydia held back tears as she stood helplessly watching her only son convulsed with fever.

"Mahayla, you are only making this worse," Summer scolded.

"I am not going to sit here and watch Charlie die! I am going to bring Papa home!" Mahayla declared as she stood up.

"How? Papa has the horse and carriage," Summer argued.

"I will borrow Uncle Danny's horse!" She ran down the back stairs, grabbed her cloak and rushed to her uncle's house located an eighth of a mile down the road.

After the war, Isaac's older brother, Daniel Miller, sold his busy lumber mill by the Saco River and built a large house between Dr. Miller's home and the family's homestead, River View Farm. Their home was filled with boarding students attending Fryeburg Academy.

She pounded on the backdoor shouting," Uncle Danny! Aunt Emily! It's Mahayla! Let me in!"

Emily, dressed in her wrap and nightclothes, opened the door.

"Charlie is dying! I must get Papa. I need to borrow your horse and ride out to Old Man Parker's house and bring him home!"

Daniel Miller, now fully dressed, entered the kitchen. "You cannot go out alone at night. You stay with Charlie, and I will go get your father," he instructed.

No one heard Jeremy Chase come down the back stairs. "Sir, please allow me to go. I know the way. You and Mrs. Miller should be with Charlie and the family."

Daniel stopped for a moment to consider the offer. "Jeremy, I will be most grateful for your help. Yes, thank you."

Grabbing his coat, hat, and lantern, the young man quickly entered the stable and saddled the horse. His heart pounded in his chest as he galloped past River View Farm, over the covered bridge crossing the Saco River, and headed towards North Fryeburg. Upon arrival at Mr. Parker's hovel, he pounded on the door shouting, "Dr. Miller! You must come home. Charlie is dying!"

The door violently opened. "How did you…"

"Mahayla sent me here. I have your brother's horse."

"I cannot leave the poor man alone to die," Isaac objected.

"He will not be alone. I will stay with him," he offered. "You are the only one who can save Charlie. I will stay. Please go home."

Isaac feared the worse when he spied Reverend Stone's carriage. Daniel greeted him at the back door. "He is still alive. Mahayla has applied a poultice for his chest to help him breathe." This was an old family recipe her grandmother taught her. She combined one cup of flour, and quarter cup of ground mustard seeds, and enough hot water to make a paste. She spread a thin

Scarlet Fever

layer of bacon grease on his chest to protect him from burns, applied the plaster and covered his chest with a warmed towel.[2]

"Lydia and Summer are combating the fever with cold, wet cloths. Emily and Pastor are praying. We are doing everything we can."

Isaac ran up the back stairs two at a time. The sight of his listless, pale, emaciated son was almost more than what he could bear. He took a deep breath. Tomorrow he could be the fretful father; tonight, he was the doctor.

———— ❋ ————

At sunrise Mahayla was in the kitchen boiling water for tea. Reverend Stone, Daniel and Emily had returned to their homes, and the rest of the family fitfully slept upstairs.

Jeremy spied Mahayla through the window and rapped on the back door. "How is Charlie?" he asked anxiously as he entered the kitchen.

"His fever broke, and he is sleeping comfortably. His breathing sounds much better."

Jeremy gave an audible sigh of relief.

"Please sit by the stove and have a cup of tea to warm you up," she offered. "How is Old Man Parker?"

"He died two hours ago. I went to the parsonage of the Unitarian Church and told the minister. He assured me that he and the deacons would plan for a funeral and burial."

"You were very brave last night."

"It was nothing," he blushed.

"It meant everything to me," she put her hand on his arm. "I will remember your kindness the rest of my life."

Suddenly Jeremy no longer felt cold and exhausted, as he took her hand into his.

Isaac was grateful when no patients arrived for morning office hours. After three hours of sleep, and two cups of coffee, he spent the morning by his son's bedside. Charlie's fever was mild, his pulse was weak, and his lungs were congested. He meticulously noted every detail into Charlie's patient file.

Lydia quietly slipped into the room. "How is he?" she whispered.

"The danger has passed. Now we wait and see."

"What do you mean?" she questioned. Both Summer and Mahayla made full recoveries. What was Isaac not telling her? "What do you mean?" she repeated.

He chose his words carefully. Isaac did not wish to frighten his wife, yet Dr. Miller was always honest with his patients. "It may take months for Charlie to recover. Some patients do not make a full recovery. We need to wait and see."

He sadly looked down at his sleeping son. "I should have been here," he silently berated himself. "I should have been here."

It was midafternoon and Mahayla was reading aloud *Around the World in Eighty Days* by Jules Verne to her sleeping brother. Suddenly he opened his eyes and whimpered, "Hayley, my throat is sore."

"I know. Would you like a cup of tea?"

"Where is Charlie? Where is my Charlie doll?" he began to cry.

During the war, Aunt Emily had sewn four rag dolls, Summer, Mahayla, Mama, and Papa. When Isaac returned home from the war with one leg amputated, Mahayla promptly cut off one of Papa Doll's legs. When Isaac purchased a prosthesis, she tied a stick onto the doll's amputated leg. Much to Isaac's dismay, three-year-old Charlie enjoyed playing with them and asked Aunt Emily to sew him a Charlie Doll. He slept with Charlie and Hayley Doll every night and took Charlie Doll everywhere with him. Four years ago, the five dolls were packed in a trunk in the attic.

He started crying louder.

Lydia ran into the room. "Charlie, are you in pain?"

Isaac followed, felt his forehead, and took his pulse. "Charlie, let me help you sit up," he rearranged the pillows. "Lydia, please bring him some broth. We need to get some fluids in him."

"No! No!" he angrily pushed his father away. "I want Charlie! Where is Charlie?"

"Son, you are Charlie. You are right here," Isaac tried to reason.

As Mahayla quietly left for the attic, she could hear her brother screaming, "I want Charlie! Charlie!" She reentered holding two dolls. "Here is Charlie," she handed him the first doll. "Hayley wanted to visit you too."

He clasped both dolls to his chest. "Why did you run away? I have been looking for you for days." He promptly fell asleep clutching both dolls.

They heard knocking on the back door and then the door opened.

"Isaac! Isaac are you home?" his oldest brother, Eli, frantically shouted.

Isaac called from the top of the stairs. "What is wrong, Eli?"

"Grab your bag and come to the farm. Ma collapsed in the kitchen. She is dying!"

II

Apoplexy

Isaac was born thirty-seven years ago in this rambling, old farmhouse. He entered the familiar kitchen with the plain, iron cookstove in the corner, and a large pine trestle table in the middle of the room. He found an overturned chair, and his elderly mother lying on the floor. His father was seated on the floor beside her. "Katie, talk to me. Talk to me," he pleaded.

Soup was bubbling in a large, iron pot. Potato peelings covered a corner of the table, and a shattered earthen ware bowl filled with diced potatoes was near the overturned chair. "She just collapsed. She was fine one minute and then she just collapsed," Eli's wife, Julia repeated. "What is wrong with her? What happened?"

Isaac knelt beside his mother and took her pulse.

"Is she going to die?" Eli asked as he ran a calloused hand through his curly gray hair. Everyone began talking at once.

"Silence!" Isaac demanded. "Everyone leave the room so I may examine my patient in peace."

Eli, who was twenty-two years older than Isaac, began to protest.

"Eli, let me do my job. Help Pa up and bring him to the dining room."

"Ma, it is Isaac." He noted that one side of her face drooped. "I know you cannot speak. If you understand me, blink."

One eye blinked.

"I need to know if you have broken any bones before I can move you. Can you nod your head?"

She nodded.

"Can you shake your head?"

She shook her head.

"Good," Isaac smiled. "Are you in pain?"

She shook her head.

"Take and squeeze my hand."

She reached with her left hand and squeezed.

"Now with your right hand."

A look of terror filled her eyes.

"I know, Ma. You are safe. Can you move your left foot? How about your right foot?"

A tear trickled down her cheek.

The family stood huddled by the door, silently watching.

"You may come in," he called over his shoulder. Isaac took his mother's left hand. "Ma, you have apoplexy.[1] It is a problem that happens with your brain. That is why you cannot move your right side. I know you can understand what I am saying. The right side of your face is paralyzed. I want you to try to talk. It will be garbled. But with practice it will improve over time."

"Ja- Ja," she croaked.

"I am here, Katie. I will never leave you." Isaac's father, Jacob, knelt by his wife's side. "I will never leave you." He promised.

"Ma, I want you to swallow for me."

She gulped.

Apoplexy

"That is very good. It is important that you can eat and drink. It will take practice. The situation is not as severe as I originally feared. Now Eli and I are going to slowly help you sit up. When we help you stand, put your weight on your left leg. Good. Now we will help you into this chair. How does that feel?"

"G-G."

"Eli, your grandmother's chair with wheels is in the spare bedroom upstairs. Bring it down," his father instructed.

"Isaac, I need your help. Come with me," Eli invited. Once upstairs he asked, "Is she going to die?"

"Eventually, but not from this. Apoplexy is not a disease. It is a symptom of a problem in her brain. Chances are it could happen again, and that could kill her."

"How can you fix it?"

"I cannot look inside of her head. If I could, perhaps I could prevent it from getting worse. All we can do is care for her and make her comfortable. You and Julia will need to move to the farm. Pa cannot care for her by himself. You are going to inherit the farm anyway. You might as well take over the farm today.

I will stop in tonight to check on her."

"You are not leaving! Where are you going?"

"I have a critical patient who needs me."

"Who is more important than your own mother?" Eli demanded.

"My son."

---❈---

Reverend Stone entered Evans General Store, where he spied Rachel Miller Evans writing in a ledger behind the counter.

"Good afternoon, Mrs. Evans," he quietly greeted.

Rachel quickly looked up and smiled. "Why Reverend, how good to see you. How may I help you today?"

"I am here to deliver a message from your brother – Dr. Miller," he clarified.

Her eyes filled with tears. "Is it Charlie? Is he… did he…?" She could not complete the question.

"No. Charlie gave us all a scare last night, but his fever broke. He is very weak, and will need weeks or months to recover."

Rachel's husband, Peter Evans, walked over to the counter. "Reverend?"

"I am afraid your mother has suddenly taken ill. Eli and Julia are moving in to help your father care for her. Julia will need all the assistance she can get from the family. I am going to inform Daniel and Emily. We cannot expect Lydia and the girls to help at this time."

"Of course. What happened?" Rachel could feel her pulse racing. Her mother, the matriarch of the Miller family, took care of everyone and everything.

"I will run the store. You take all the time you need," Peter reassured.

"What happened?" she repeated.

"I am afraid it is apoplexy."

"Mama!" Rachel ran into the front parlor of the farmhouse, where she found her mother seated in her grandmother's wheeled chair. She was silently looking out the window, staring at her beloved gardens. Jacob, sitting beside her, protectively

Apoplexy

held her left hand. He silently turned his head and sadly looked at his only daughter.

Rachel knelt beside her mother. "Oh, Mama," she put her head on Kate's lap as she quietly wept. The elderly woman patted her daughter's head with her left hand, and silently stared out the window.

Daniel and Emily quietly entered the farmhouse kitchen, where they found Eli and Julia sitting at the pine trestle table. This was a family heirloom built with patriotic defiance by their great-grandfather, James Miller, in 1776. When he and the town of Fryeburg had learned the thirteen colonies had declared their independence, he took his ax, and headed to the woods toward the King's Pine. The agents of King George III had marked this huge tree with the king's broad arrow, reserving it to be cut only for a mast in his majesty's navy. That day King George lost a tree, and the Millers had lumber for a new table.

Julia looked up. "One minute she was fine. The next minute she collapsed on the floor."

"It was a blessing that you were with her," Emily consoled. "If she was alone, she could have lain there for hours."

"Reverend Stone stopped by our house and told us what happened. How may we help? Do you need help with the plowing? The planting? Emily will stop by every day to help care for mother," Daniel offered.

"Isaac told me we should move in," Eli began, hoping his resentment would not be noticed.

"I agree. The time is long overdue. You are going to inherit the farm. Does it not make sense you move in now when you are most needed?"

"Have you been talking to Isaac again?" Eli accused.

"Not recently. Not since Charlie took sick. We almost lost him last night."

"We had no idea!" Julia gasped. "Poor Lydia! Why did he not tell us?"

"It was time to be a doctor, and not a brother. We cannot expect Lydia and the girls to help. These responsibilities will fall to the four of us," Daniel explained.

"You mean the five of us," Rachel corrected, as she entered the kitchen carrying a half empty teacup.

"Yes, the five of us," Daniel agreed. Eli looked away saying nothing.

———❋———

It was the last week of May when the ground was dry enough to begin planting. Eli, eager to be outside ploughing the fields, was not pleased to be dressing into his Sunday suit. His brothers had badgered him for weeks about the farm. It was his sister who secretly discussed the plan to his parents. Jacob eagerly agreed and Kate nodded in approval.

"Eli, you are keeping your father waiting," Julia crossly reminded him. The past six weeks had been a difficult transition. She reluctantly left her tidy home filled with memories of raising her son and two daughters. Everything had been organized according to her preferences. Then she left it all behind – her furniture, her dishes, her pots, and pans to move into this old, drafty house furnished with four generations of other people's possessions and memories. Although her house was only a walk across the bridge, it felt a world away. Now her older daughter, Becky, her son-in-law, Jonathan with their five children will move into her home.

Apoplexy

"As of today, you shall be the mistress of River View Farm," Eli turned to his wife.

"Mistress, until your sister comes and takes over every day," she thought but wisely said nothing.

Jacob, also dressed in his Sunday best, paced the parlor floor. "Sit!" Kate scolded.

"Katie, dear, you spoke so clearly!" he beamed with pride as he sat beside her. "You are improving every day. Last night you ate the entire meal with your left hand and did not spill one drop."

She sadly stared out the window at her garden.

"Pa, the wagon is ready," Eli announced.

"You must not keep Attorney Hastings waiting," Julia hoped she sounded cheerful. Yet, she realized her life would change forever with a stroke of a pen.

———❋———

"No, Isaac. He is not ready!"

"Lydia, Charlie has not been outside in months. He needs the fresh air and sunshine," he sternly replied. "I am his doctor and I say a few hours outdoors at the farm will do good."

"Mama, you know he is getting bored being cooped up all day. You will have some peace and quiet while you work," Summer pleasantly reminded.

"I am not a baby!" Charlie screamed. "I will not ride in that stupid, old wagon."

"It is not for you. It is for Charlie Doll," Mahayla carefully placed the rag doll in the center of the wagon. "Come on!" she left the yard pulling the wagon behind her. Charlie cautiously followed her.

After fifty steps, Charlie was out of breath. "Charlie Doll is scared. He needs me to ride with him."

"Well, that is very thoughtful of you. Get in."

Charlie waved at Daniel's house as they passed by. When they pulled up to the farm a look of recognition crossed his face, and he smiled a crooked smile.

They entered the front parlor and found Kate sitting in her wheeled chair staring out the window while Jacob dozed in the wing backed chair.

"Nana, we are here to work in the gardens," Mahayla announced.

Jacob awoke with a start. Kate looked confused.

"Da- Da-vid?"

"Katie, dear. Our David is gone. Remember his beautiful funeral? This is our youngest grandson, Charlie. He has been very sick, and this is his first visit in a long time."

Since their granddaughter, Becky, moved into her parent's home two weeks ago, the farmhouse was filled with activity. This oldest granddaughter had two teenage boys who visited daily to work on the farm. With these great grandsons, their sisters, and six-year-old brother, plus Rachel and Emily coming and going throughout the day, Kate often grew exhausted and confused.

"Charlie, come give your old grandfather a hug!"

"Charlie Doll wants a hug too!" he handed his treasured possession to his grandfather. Jacob looked bewildered, for this was not the same child he had last seen several months ago.

Mahayla shrugged and smiled helplessly. "Nana let me take you outside to the gardens and you can watch us work."

"Yes! Yes! Out." She excitedly pointed to the window. Jacob parked the wheeled chair in a shady spot while Mahayla began weeding. Charlie soon fell asleep on the grass in the sunshine.

It was a daily routine that lasted throughout the summer, until one morning in September.

"Katie, it is getting late. Let me help you get up. Everyone has had breakfast and Mahayla and Charlie will be here any minute. Katie. Katie!"

"Eli!" Jacob yelled. "Eli, get your brother!"

Eli ran into the bedroom and stared at his mother. "Pa, we don't need a doctor. She's dead."

III

A Busy Sunday

Dr. Miller and his entire family promptly entered Fryeburg's Congregational Church for the first time in months. Isaac looked distinguished in his black three-piece suit, and streaks of gray in his dark beard and curly hair. His grandfather's cane and slight limp betrayed his amputated left leg and prosthesis.

Lydia walked down the aisle by his side with the swishing of her petticoats. She wore the tightest corset and the largest bustle in the town of Fryeburg. Her large, brimmed hat was securely placed on her upswept, auburn hair with two large hat pins.

Summer demurely walked behind her parents. Most of the young men at Fryeburg Academy agreed she was a beauty with her auburn hair, green eyes, and fair complexion. She was elegantly dressed in one of her mother's outfits, hat, heels, and gloves. Both ladies were dressed in black.

It was a beautiful, warm September morning, and Mahayla eschewed the bustle, the gloves, and layers of petticoats. She wore a simple, dark, cotton dress with one sensible cotton petticoat. Her dark brown, wavy hair was tied back with a ribbon. Much to her mother's chagrin, she often did not wear a bonnet while gardening, and her face and hands were deeply tanned.

The old timers thought she resembled her great-grandmother, Hannah Miller, in appearance, but not in demeanor. This outspoken and assertive girl was nothing like her quiet, Quaker ancestor. She lovingly held her younger brother's hand.

Breaking free from his sister's grasp, Charlie ran up the aisle to the second, center pew yelling, "Grandpa! Grandpa!" Jacob turned around and put his finger to his lips. His grandson eagerly sat in the empty space in the pew and leaned his head on his beloved grandfather's shoulder. The rest of the family took their places.

"Nana can't come to church today because she is in heaven. They put her in a box and sent her to heaven. Will Jesus take her out of the box?" he asked Pastor Stone in a loud voice.

Half the church shook their heads in dismay. "You can put a tweed suit on the village idiot, but he's still an idiot!"

The more compassionate half of the church smiled sadly. Jacob Miller had suffered so much loss in recent years. He lost two grandsons and almost lost Isaac during the war, and now his beloved wife.

Eventually Charlie settled down sitting between his grandfather and Uncle Danny. He stared into space with his head tilted to the left and his mouth slightly opened, as he quietly listened to the sermon. When the organ began to play, he stood with the congregation, took out his hymnal and sang *How Great Thou Art* with the voice of an angel. It did not matter that the hymnal was upside down and turned to the wrong page.

"Father Miller, please join us for Sunday dinner. It has been a trying week, and you need to eat and rest," Lydia invited. She knew Julia invited her daughter Becky, her husband and five children to Sunday dinner every week.

One look into Charlie's pleading, brown eyes and Jacob accepted the invitation with a forced smile. Daniel and Emily helped him into their carriage as the rest of the family walked down the main street to Isaac's home.

Although Jacob was born on the farm, he spent most of his childhood and young adult life in this house. When he entered the front foyer, he silently noted all the redecorating Lydia had completed in a few short years.

His father's large law office to the right was transformed into four smaller rooms for his son's medical practice. The front room served as the patients' waiting room. Isaac had two small examining rooms and a large office with bookcases holding his medical books, a microscope, and stoneware jugs filled with the newest medicines, bottles, and corks.

All the majestic pine posts and beams, so expertly crafted by his Uncle Ethan, were now hidden behind plaster and covered with wallpaper. Pressed tin ceilings in every room hid the original wooden ones. Plush carpeting, manufactured in Maine textile mills, covered the wide planked oak floors. Heavy draperies darkened the once sun-lit rooms.

He quietly sat in the front parlor with his two sons, while the ladies reheated a pot of baked beans, made tea, and set the table with new, blue willow ware china. He wondered what happened to his mother's plain, white china rimmed with gold. He had fond memories of family meals with those dishes.

Loud knocking on the front door interrupted his brooding thoughts. Lydia frowned at the thought of another family meal interrupted by an emergency. Isaac opened the front door.

"Isaac, Aunt Harriet wishes you to visit her this afternoon after your dinner," his cousin George informed him.

"Is she ill?"

"Heavens no! She will outlive us all! Her gout and rheumatism kept her homebound, and she is upset about missing your mother's funeral. She insists she must talk to you today before she dies, which according to her is any day now. Of course, she has been saying that for the past twenty years."

"It is a lovely day for a ride and please tell her I am delighted to accept the invitation." Aunt Harriet was his favorite aunt.

The family quietly and wearily began their modest lunch. "The new instructor at Fryeburg Academy will be boarding with us this school year" Daniel broke the silence. "Emily arranged a corner of the third floor into a comfortable bedroom/ sitting room."

"I think having both students and an instructor under your roof this year will be interesting." Lydia politely stated.

"Papa, may I accompany you to visit Aunt Harriet?" Mahayla asked.

"I am sure Aunt Harriet would appreciate the visit and I would enjoy the company," Isaac agreed.

"Mahayla, I need you to help your sister clean the kitchen," Lydia reminded.

"Charlie can wash the dishes. He is not stupid."

Charlie perked up. "Hayley is right. I'm not stupid. I can wash the dishes."

"I do not wish for him to overtire and have a relapse," Lydia fretted.

"I believe he is capable of helping around the house," Isaac contradicted.

"I can do it. Hayley says I can. I'm not stupid. I can do it. I can…"

"That is enough, Charlie," Isaac scolded.

Daniel returned his father to River View Farm, as Summer and an excited Charlie cleaned the kitchen. Mahayla helped her father hitch the horse to the carriage, and leisurely headed toward North Fryeburg.

"Papa, I have decided that I shall become a doctor."

"You mean a nurse like Clara Barton," he corrected.

"No, I mean I want to become a doctor like Elizabeth and Emily Blackwell."

"Who?"

"Elizabeth Blackwell is the first woman in the United States to become a doctor. Several years later, her sister Emily also became a doctor. The two of them established a rigorous medical school for women and an infirmary in New York City.[1] I believe women and children would respond more favorably to a woman doctor. Don't you?"

"Have you been talking to your Aunt Rachel?"

"Aunt Rachel believes women should vote. Nana believed women could become doctors."

"Did she, now?"

"She also said that I am much more mature and dependable than you when you were my age."

"Good grief!"

"Hello, Aunt Harriet," Isaac greeted the ninety-year-old woman sitting in a wing back chair with her feet propped up on a foot stool.

A Busy Sunday

"This is a social visit and not a house call. I am not paying for this visit," she warned.

"No, Mam," he smiled.

"Aunt Harriet, you are looking well today," Mahayla complimented.

"Young lady, are you still getting in trouble in school?"

"Yes, I am. Thank you for asking," she stifled a laugh.

"Please go to the kitchen and make a pot of tea. I wish to speak to your father in private."

"Yes, mam."

"Isaac, you were your mother's favorite."

"According to my brother, Eli, I am."

"She was concerned about you. Charlie is not your fault."

"If I had been home, I could have prevented the convulsions. I fear he will never make a full recovery. What kind of father am I? What kind of doctor am I?"

"You are a good father and a good doctor, but you are not God. Remember that."

"Yes, mam."

"How is your father holding up?"

"As well as can be expected."

"Kate was an exceptional woman and farmer's wife. There was nothing she could not do. She was the rock of Gibraltar, and the one who held the family together. I do not know how your father will manage without her."

"You know that Eli and Julia moved into the farm to care for them. My cousin Becky and family moved into Eli's house to help run the farm. Danny and I live nearby. The family will all help."

"Your mother worried about you after Davy and Darian died. You took their deaths awfully hard."

"Thousands of men died in battle. I could accept that. But Davy died at home."

"You know he was not right in the head. What was he thinking going up to that hayloft in the middle of the night?"

Isaac stiffened and clenched his jaw. "Like you said, he was not right in the head. He may have thought he was guarding the barn from invading Rebels. And Darian died in Andersonville Prison on the very day the war ended. We all took their deaths hard. My father still has not recovered from losing them."

"Finally, here is my tea. Mahayla, dear, please join us."

"I did it! Summer helped, but I did it," Charlie proudly announced. "I'm not stupid."

"Yes, you did. You look tired. Do you need to lay down?" Lydia asked.

"Charlie Doll and I will take a nap."

"Summer, what a pleasant surprise. Do come in," Rachel invited her niece into the second-floor apartment above their General Store.

"Aunt Rachel, I am sorry for your loss. How are you holding up?"

"Exhausted, like everyone else. It has been a difficult year, but this family has survived worse."

"Like the war?"

"Let us not dwell on our problems on such a beautiful afternoon. I have not had the opportunity to sit and talk to you for months. You are entering your last year at the Academy. Do you have plans?"

"Yes. I want to become a writer. Look at the impact Harriet Beecher Stowe had, when she published *Uncle Tom's Cabin*. President Lincoln told her, 'So you are the little woman who wrote the book that started this great war.'"[1.]

"Yes, women writers can change opinions. You will not be the first writer in the family. You must read Aunt Grace's stories."

"Who?"

"Grace Peabody married your great-grandfather's brother, Micah Miller, lived and raised her family at River View Farm. She and your great-grandmother, Hannah Miller, were the best of friends. Aunt Grace died the year before you were born. During the last years of her life, she wrote four journals – a history of our family and the town of Fryeburg. Danny owns them now and he wrote a fifth story about our family during the War."

"Really? May I read them?"

"Of course. You may continue where Aunt Grace and Danny left off. What do you want to write about?"

"First, I want to write a novel about a girl who left the farm to work in a textile mill."

"I worked in a textile mill before I married Uncle Peter."

"I know. That is why I am here to interview you. Do you think I can do it?" Summer asked.

"We Miller ladies can do anything we put our minds to. Remember that."

IV

The Amputation

Isaac and Mahayla were chuckling about their visit as they headed home. "It is good to see you laugh, Papa. You do not smile anymore. Aunt Harriet is right. Charlie's illness is not your fault."

"Laughter is good medicine," he agreed. "It is easy to forget all the good things in life when you are surrounded by illness, accidents, and deaths night and day."

"Like the war?"

"Yes."

"I remember the day you came home from the war without your leg. But I cannot remember you before the war."

"You were too young."

"I remember my cousin Davy when he returned from the war. He was strange, but good and kind, at the same time. You were never the same after Davy died. You acted like his accident was your fault, like Charlie's illness."

"You are an insightful young woman," he complimented.

"Doctors need to be insightful," she reminded.

"Yes, they do."

Their conversation was interrupted by the pounding of hooves behind them. "Dr. Miller! Thank God you are here!" The horse came to an abrupt stop beside the carriage.

"Jeremy, what is wrong?"

"My father was kicked by a horse. His leg is shattered. The bone is sticking out. There is blood everywhere."

"Tell your mother to begin boiling pots of water and to gather clean sheets and rags. I know where you live. I will be right behind you." Jeremy turned the horse around and galloped toward home. "This is why I always carry my bags with me."

Dr. Miller owned two large, black leather valises. In the first bag, he carried his stethoscope, a new glass thermometer carefully wrapped in cloth, a bottle of witch hazel, assorted teas, vials of medicine, a glass syringe, and a small bottle of morphine. His surgical bag contained a bone saw, scalpels, blades, needles, cat gut sutures, rags, a bottle of chloroform, and a leather apron.

Upon arriving at the modest farm, Dr. Miller grabbed both bags and hurried to the barn where Mrs. Chase was desperately trying to console her husband. The doctor took off his jacket, rolled up his sleeves, and knelt by the patient, silently studying the shattered leg.

"Well George, this looks serious. Jeremy and Mahayla, please take down the bedroom door and bring it here. We will use it like a litter to bring him to the kitchen table. Mrs. Chase, please clear off the table and cover it with a sheet and bring another sheet."

Now alone with his patient, he shook his head as he inspected the injury. The tibia was hopelessly shattered. The wound was impacted with filth and manure from the bottom of the horse's hoof. Amputation was the only option to prevent the spread of infection and save this hardworking farmer's life.

Jeremy and Mahayla carried in the door. "Please place it by his side. Hand me that plank," he nodded to the short board laying on its side in the corner. "Mrs. Chase, please drape the sheet over the door. I will slide the plank under the injured leg." The four of them gingerly placed the patient on the door. "Each of us will take one corner of the door. Now on my count lift the door and slowly head for the house."

Everyone remained silent as they focused transporting the patient out of the barn, up the back stairs, and into the kitchen. "Now we will place the door on the kitchen table."

With his patient carefully situated, he turned to the family. "I am going to tell you the truth. This is a serious injury."

Jeremy pulled out a kitchen chair. "Have a seat, Ma."

"There is no way I can save the leg," he stated softly as he looked directly into Mrs. Chase's eyes. "The only way I can save his life is to amputate. We must avoid infection at all costs. During the war, more men died of infections from their wounds, than from their wounds. I will show you how to clean and dress the wound and I promise I will come daily to care for him as well."

"There is no other way?" Mrs. Chase asked in a whisper.

"There is no other way. George, I am going to give you something so you will not feel pain while I am working on your leg. Mahayla, please get the chloroform and rag."

"Not ether?"

"Ether never leaves my office. It is too unstable and volatile," he explained as he carefully put a few drops of chloroform on the rag. "Now George, take a couple of deep breaths.

I cannot promise he will survive. I do promise that I will do everything in my power to save his life. Once the danger has passed, we will discuss purchasing a prosthesis.

I need four of your largest pots filled with boiling water. Mahayla, we need to scrub our hands with plenty of soap." They both rolled up their sleeves above the elbows.

"Why?" Jeremy asked.

"Dr. Joseph Lister, a surgeon in Scotland, proposes heat kills germs that cause infections. You cannot see germs with your eyes, but you can under some microscopes.[2]

I have witnessed soldiers die after successful surgeries, because the instruments, the doctors, the surroundings were filthy. I had my leg amputated in a crowded, dirty barn with bloody instruments. Patients were lying on the ground. I promised myself that I will devote as much care before the surgery as during.

Jeremy, please take your mother outside to select a proper burial spot for the leg. It should be far from your well and garden area. Then dig a hole three feet deep and three feet long. Mahayla will bring the limb wrapped in a sheet out to you."

"Yes, sir," Jeremy solemnly replied. Mahayla saw the fear in his eyes.

Isaac waited for the mother and son to leave the house, and walk to the far end of their property with shovel in hand. He turned to his daughter. "After today, you will know if you still wish to be a doctor."

While the bone saw is in the boiling water, we need to determine the point of amputation." He took out his stethoscope. "I need to find a strong pulse in the leg."

He took his stethoscope, a long wooden tube, and placed it near the surgical site. "It is vital for the leg to have a pulse before I begin amputating." Next, he felt the injured leg above the surgical site and the uninjured leg. "I am comparing the skin temperatures of both legs. This tells me that the blood is circulating just above where I intend to operate."

Mahayla was impressed with her father's calm demeanor and thoroughness.

"Hand me that sheet." He placed it under the lower section of the leg. "Stand back. This will be fast. When I'm done, wrap the limb in the sheet and place it out on the porch." He grabbed the sterilized bone saw and took a deep breath.

Mahayla was amazed how fast he cut off the leg. Would she ever have the physical strength and agility to accomplish such a feat?

Isaac loudly exhaled before removing any diseased tissue and crushed bone. With the skill of carpenter sanding a fine piece of furniture, he smoothed all the uneven areas of the bone.

"Hand me the cat gut sutures and needle." He meticulously sealed off the blood vessels and nerves."

"Now what are you doing?" Mahayla asked in fascination.

"I am cutting and shaping the muscles, so he can have a prosthesis, if he chooses. And now I will sew the skin flaps over it. [3.]

"Mahayla, please boil some more water, wash all the instruments, and throw the bloody rags into the cookstove. Mrs. Chase does not need to see the aftermath." As Mahayla was cleaning, Isaac took his stethoscope to listen to the pulse of the leg and the heart. He noted with satisfaction that both were strong.

Once the kitchen was scrubbed and the hole was dug, Isaac instructed, "Bring the limb out for burial. Ask Jeremy to take you home. It will be getting dark soon and your mother will worry. Have Jeremy ask Reverend Stone, Uncle Danny, and Aunt Emily to come. I will need the men's help to get my patient properly placed into bed and I want Emily to keep Mrs. Chase company."

After burying the limb, Jeremy took Mahayla home. No one spoke,

Mahayla found supper being reheated as she entered the kitchen. "You are late, very late. Charlie Doll was getting worried," Charlie scolded.

"Mr. Chase had a very serious accident. Jeremy brought me home and Papa will be spending the night there. I am not hungry. I am going to bed."

Isaac was grateful for everyone's assistance last night. The surgery proceeded as well as could be expected. With his patient settled in his bed and mercifully sedated, he left the farm with promises of returning late in the afternoon.

As he returned, he thought, "Perhaps Aunt Harriet was right; I take too much responsibility upon myself. But these people are not just patients, they are friends and family. They depend on me. When I fail, I grieve with their families.

Aunt Harriet was right. I was my mother's favorite. I spent hours working in her herb gardens. She taught me everything I know about compounding medicine. When I was a failure of a farmer, a husband and father, she never gave up on me. She sold her successful creamery business and used the funds to purchase my prosthesis and begin my apothecary business. She believed in me when I no longer believed in myself. It was because of her, I had the confidence and knowledge to earn a medical degree at Bowdoin College.

Then she had apoplexy and there was nothing I could do to make her well. Now she is gone. I should have been a better doctor. I should have been a better son.

Aunt Harriet was right about everything."

V

Mr. Bennett

As Emerson Bennett stepped down from the train at the Fryeburg depot, he observed the wagons and carriages picking up passengers. He took out the directions from his jacket pocket, and began walking past a large fairground, and up Smith Street. As he approached Main Street, he saw a large four-story, yellow hotel with a long addition containing stables with rooms above. A well- dressed clientele entered and exited the premises. Several carriages were stopped by the front door where porters were carrying trunks, and hat boxes, and assisting ladies with voluminous dresses, and large feathered hats down from their carriages.

Across the street from the hotel was a large general store filled with customers donned in more practical and modest attire. The street was lined with elm trees which provided shade for the private homes and businesses. He passed a stone schoolhouse and a small brick Registry of Deeds building, before crossing the busy street in front of a large white house on the corner of Main and Bridge Street. He knew this was the side street which led to his new home.

He was rather pleased when he stopped in front of the white, three-story house and walked to the front door with anticipation. Daniel answered. "Mr. Bennett, do come in. We have been expecting you."

"You must be Mr. Miller. It is a pleasure to make your acquaintance," he shook Daniel's hand.

Emily quietly entered the foyer and studied the tall, slender, bespeckled, young man dressed in a fine, though dusty, three-piece, wool suit and white, silk shirt. He held his top hat in one hand, and a black leather valise in the other. "Welcome to our home, Mr. Bennett. Let us show you the first floor, before we show you to your quarters on the third floor. Your three trunks arrived last week."

"You see we have two front parlors. The one on the right is reserved for members of the Miller family. The other is for our boarders, visiting family, and guests. We want our boarders to feel their friends and family are welcomed anytime," Daniel explained. "We have three downstair bedrooms. Our bedroom is the one in the front of the house. The other two are reserved for our friends who may need accommodations. Presently we have no one staying with us."

"Here is our dining room," Emily led him into a large room with several windows facing west to River View Farm and the Saco River.

"It looks like a restaurant in Boston," he marveled at the four rectangular tables, two sideboards filled with plates, platters, teacups, glasses, and silverware.

"One table will suffice this week. We need all four tables for Miller family celebrations," Emily explained. "We need three tables during the winter months when we have more boarders.

Our Academy students often come here in the evenings to study by the warmth of the parlor stove.

And finally, here is the kitchen." The room was equipped with a soapstone sink and hand pump, a large Glenwood cookstove, and a small icebox which stood in the corner beside a large pantry. "No one enters my kitchen unless they are prepared to wash dishes, or cook meals," she teased good naturedly.

"Let us show you to your living quarters on the third floor. On the second floor, we have two large rooms with six beds and dressers in each for our Fryeburg Academy students. This weekend we are expecting two students from East Fryeburg and one from North Fryeburg. We will have more boarders as winter approaches."

As they climbed the stairs Emily explained, "You are the first guest we have staying on this floor. Mr. Miller and I agreed that living on the second floor with several boisterous young men may be a distraction, and you needed more private quarters. I do hope you will find it to your liking," she opened the door to a large, corner room.

Mr. Bennett surveyed the small bed covered with a quilt made of large blue, green, and white squares and a small bedstand with a lamp. A large pine armoire was placed between two windows. A pine desk stood in front of a third window offering a view of a neighboring farm. A small settee was placed under the fourth window. A large bookcase sat between these two windows. Three trunks were placed on a large, braided rug in the center of the room. White lace curtains hung in the windows. Several paintings of local landscapes adorned the plain white walls.

"Mr. and Mrs. Miller, these accommodations far exceed my expectations. Who painted these lovely pictures?

"Sadie Miller, my father's cousin, painted these forty years ago."

"Who owns the farm?" Mr. Bennett pointed to the window.

"That is River View Farm, the Miller homestead. My father lives there with my older brother and sister-in-law."

"Who lives in that magnificent house on the corner?"

"My younger brother, Dr. Isaac Miller, his wife, and children. Although you may hear the old timers refer to it as the Senator Benjamin Miller House."

"Your family is related to Senator Miller? I read about him in college."

"He was my grandfather," Daniel proudly replied.

"Mr. and Mrs. Miller, thank you for everything. I do have one question. Where is the Unitarian Church?"

That question displeased them. Fryeburg originally had only one church, the Congregational Church. Fryeburg Academy was historically tied with the Congregational Church. Then the Unitarian Church was established in the 1820's and they built a meeting house in North Fryeburg.

Back in '53 after the death of Benjamin Miller, the head Trustee of the Academy, there was a serious quarrel. Reverend Hurd insisted that any Headmaster at the Academy must be a graduate of the more conservative Theological Institute at Andover. However, Major James Osgood, a Unitarian, put his son in.[3] There has been underlying tension ever since.

"Oh, you are a Unitarian, sir?"

"The Bennett family has been prominent members of the First Parish in Concord, Massachusetts for four generations. My grandfather was very close friends with Reverend Ezra Ripley." He noted the lack of name recognition on their faces. "Reverend

Ripley was highly esteemed in Concord and throughout the Boston area."

"I fear North Fryeburg is much too far to walk. However, I am sure Mr. Osgood would give you a ride in his carriage. Of course, you are always welcome to come to church with us" Daniel warmly invited.

"Thank you. I am most grateful for such superb accommodations with such a distinguished family. I will unpack before I take a walk to the Academy. I am looking forward to meeting the rest of your family."

He devoted the next two hours, organizing his precious books and his papers. He hung his clothing in his armoire, before writing two letters to home back in Concord. He took some paper, ink, and fountain pen, sat at his desk, and penned a letter.

Dear Mother,

I am writing to assure you that I am not living in "the forsaken wilderness" nor at "the edge of civilization." The Miller home could rival many of the finer homes in Concord, and the Millers are a very distinguished family descended from Senator Benjamin Miller.

My spacious living quarters are better than I hoped, with everything I need including privacy, peace, and quiet that I require. From my windows I can gaze upon lovely pastoral scenes.

My trunks of books and clothing safely arrived last week. Later today I hope to inspect my office and classroom at the academy.

The town made a fine first impression as I strolled from the railroad station through the village to my new home. Apparently both the railroad and the telegraph office are quite new. According to a loquacious train conductor, the railroad transformed commerce to the town, and it is now thriving. Several shops and large white houses line the main street of the village. The elm trees provide shade for the pedestrians and a sense of tranquility. The Oxford House appears to be a fine establishment. Perhaps you and Lily can rent rooms there when you come to visit. The busiest enterprise is Evans' General Store. I understand they sell paper, writing supplies and even books.

I have been told the town is quite proud of their annual agricultural fair, and I will be expected to attend every year. That may prove to be interesting. It appears that the Congregational Church is the prominent church in town, although there is a Unitarian Church several miles away.

Mother, I understand that my leaving has been difficult, and you would prefer I be working at Bennett Publishing. However, I am most hopeful that I will be successful in my endeavors here in Fryeburg, and I will make you proud. They are not so "backward" after all.

You are most welcome to come for a visit. I will make this letter brief for there is much to do.

I did want to write as soon as I arrived because I know how you worry.

Your dutiful son,
Emerson

My Dearest Lily,

I am most vexed to have left you under the most distressing circumstances. Please do not be cross with me. Your father has forbidden our engagement until "I become a man worthy of his daughter."

With my humble living arrangements, I will save most of my salary for our future – to purchase a home. A few years of teaching *experience will enable me to apply for a more lucrative and prominent teaching position.*

Every decision I have made, I have made for the benefit of our future together.

Passionately,
Emerson

He briefly looked out the window and spied a young woman standing in a garden talking with an elderly man when a boy ran out of the barn.

Charlie screamed, "Chickens are bad! Chickens are very, very bad!"

"What happened?" Mahayla tried to conceal her exasperation.

"Hayley, chickens are bad. They tried to eat me!"

Eli Miller followed his nephew to the garden. "That is quite enough, young man," he warned sternly. "Chickens are not trying to eat you. You dropped the bag of seed on your foot, and they ran to eat it. What do you expect? Now come back to the barn and clean up the mess you made."

"No! The chickens will eat me! You are a bad uncle, a very bad uncle. I like Uncle Danny better!" Charlie bolted up the street crying.

"I am sorry, Uncle Eli. I will go get him." Mahayla watched her brother run to Uncle Danny's house.

Emerson Bennett knocked on the kitchen door before poking his head into the room. "Please forgive me for interrupting your sewing," he apologized.

"Not at all, do come in." Emily noticed he had changed his clothing into a more sensible cotton trousers and white shirt.

"After I post these letters, I plan to visit the academy. Is it far? I did not see it from my walk from the train station."

"It is on the same side of the street as the stone schoolhouse and general store. Continue to walk and cross Portland Street. Many shops, industries and homes are located down that street. You will pass Dr. Lamson's home where the telegraph office is located and then the Congregational Church. After a few more houses you will cross Bradley Street, and then the Academy. Enjoy your walk. Supper will be served promptly at five o'clock."

"Thank you, Mam."

Charlie burst through the kitchen door screaming, "Chickens are bad! Chickens are very bad. Horses are good but chickens are bad!" He stopped his tirade when he noticed a surprised Mr. Bennett standing by the ice box. "Aunt Emily, who is he?" he pointed to the stranger.

"Please allow me to introduce myself. Emerson James Bennett, at your service." He bowed with a flourish.

"Benjamin Charles Miller." He replied staring at the stranger. Mahayla entered the back door as Charlie stated, "Your nose looks like a chicken beak! Chickens are bad!"

"Charlie!" Mahayla gasped.

Daniel quickly entered the kitchen. "What is all this commotion?"

"Uncle Danny, chickens are bad. Uncle Eli says they are good, but he is wrong. They tried to eat me. That man's nose looks like a chicken beak!"

"Charlie, go to the front parlor and wait for me!" Daniel commanded. Charlie ignored him, staring at the stranger's nose. "Now!"

"Chickens are bad, very, very bad," he whispered as he left for the front parlor.

"Mr. Bennett, I do ask for your forgiveness at my nephew's outburst. I fear it has been a difficult year. My mother passed away last week, and you find us all in an unsettled state," Daniel apologized.

"Please accept my sincerest condolences for your loss. It is I who should apologize for arriving at such an inopportune time."

"Excuse me, I need to have a talk with Charlie," Daniel left the kitchen.

Mr. Bennett turned to Mahayla. "By the family resemblance, shall I assume you are Charlie's sister?" She nodded.

"I am so sorry for the loss of your grandmother."

"Thank you. Aunt Emily, Nana left her herb gardens to me in her will."

"A very wise choice," Emily agreed. "Mr. Bennett, this is our niece, Mahayla Miller."

"A pleasure to meet you, although I do wish it were under more pleasant circumstances. Are you the daughter of Dr. Miller?"

"Yes, sir."

"I noticed you hard at work in the gardens at your grandfather's farm. I have a lovely view of the farm, fields, and river from my desk. Are those your grandmother's herb gardens?"

"Yes, sir."

"Mahayla, Mr. Bennett is boarding with us for the school year while he is teaching literature, Latin and Greek at the Academy."

"Perhaps you are enrolled in one of my classes?"

"I have not given school much thought. I have more important matters on my mind. I fear it will be impossible to harvest all the herbs and make Nana's remedies by next week. I do not need to read Shakespeare or Ivanhoe to become a doctor."

"Are you familiar with Dr. Elizabeth Blackwell?"

"Yes, sir. I hope to attend her medical school in New York."

"Shakespeare may not be your cup of tea, but how is your Latin?"

"I have not studied Latin, sir."

"A medical student should have at least four years of Latin. You must enroll in my Latin I class. Do you wish to become a doctor like your father?"

"My desire for healing the sick comes from my grandmother. She would have been a superb doctor. I want to cure or prevent diseases like rheumatic fever and scarlet fever so children will not be stricken like Charlie. I fear he will never fully recover. He is not the same brother he was before his illness."

Daniel and a repentant Charlie entered the kitchen. "Mr. Bennett, I am very sorry that your nose looks like a chicken beak."

Daniel shook his head in despair, but Mr. Bennett chuckled. "Charlie, I would very much like to meet these chickens."

"You may join us," Daniel invited. "We are on our way to the farm to apologize to Uncle Eli. Mahayla, you are free to work in the gardens until dark. Charlie will spend the rest of the day helping me with chores at the house."

"The Millers are certainly an interesting family," he thought as he walked to the farm.

Mahayla returned to work in the gardens, and Charlie tentatively entered the barn looking for the dangerous chickens.

"Eli!" Daniel beckoned his brother. "I would like to introduce you to Mr. Emerson Bennett, the new literature and language instructor at the Academy. He is boarding with us for the school year."

"A pleasure to meet you, Mr. Miller," Mr. Bennett shook the farmer's large, callous hand.

"Charlie has something to say to you, Eli," Daniel prompted.

"I am very sorry that I said that your chickens are bad, and that you are a bad uncle. But I do like Uncle Danny much better."

Mr. Bennett

"Apology accepted. Everyone likes Uncle Danny better. I can live with that."

"I came to meet the offending chickens, and to see for myself if my nose indeed looks like a chicken's beak," Mr. Bennett explained. "Mr. Miller, may I closely examine one of your hens?"

Eli handed him a displeased hen.

"What breed is this?"

"It is a Plymouth Rock."

"Well Charlie I must disagree with you. This chicken is not bad. If fact she is rather pretty in a chicken sort of way. However, I do see a slight resemblance between my nose and her beak. I am quite fond of my beak – I mean nose–for it does an adequate job in holding up my glasses. Have I met the entire Miller family?"

Eli laughed. "Hardly. My father is in the house resting. My wife Julia and I live here. My daughter Becky, her husband, Jonathan and their five children live in the house just across the river. Jonathan and Becky help on the farm. My younger daughter and family moved to Portland. We have one sister, Rachel. She and her husband, Peter Evans, own the general store. Their sons own a business in Connecticut. When you include all the Wileys from my mother's side, the Fryes on my wife's side, the Walkers on Emily's side and of course the Evans clan, you are talking about several hundred relatives. Fortunately, they do not all live in Fryeburg."

"Well, I am looking forward to getting to know you. Now, if you gentlemen will excuse me, I have letters to mail on my way to the academy."

Emerson Bennett tried not to stare at the beautiful young woman carrying a bundle of fabric leaving Evans General Store. He tipped his hat, "Good afternoon, Miss."

"Good afternoon, sir," she replied as she kept walking. Summer was accustomed to men's admiring glances and paid no attention to the tall, awkward looking stranger.

He entered the store, and looked around at the eclectic collection of merchandise, as a middle- aged woman approached him.

"How may I help you, sir?"

One glance at the woman's dark brown curly hair and gray eyes and he surmised she must be Daniel's sister and Charlie's aunt. The Millers do resemble each other. "Madam, may I assume you are Rachel Miller Evans?"

"Have we met?" she asked in surprise.

"No, but I have had the pleasure of meeting Mr. and Mrs. Daniel Miller, Mahayla and Charlie, Eli Miller, and several chickens. I do see a strong resemblance. To the Millers, not the chickens," he quickly qualified.

Rachel smiled. "And you must be the new boarder and instructor, Mr. Bennett. I am indeed Mrs. Evans. How may I help you?"

"I am interested in perusing your writing supplies."

"Let me show you," she led him to some shelves near a display of books.

"I see you sell books as well. Does Fryeburg have a library?"

"Not yet. My niece would like to start one."

"Mahayla?"

"No, her sister, Summer. I will let you look around." She left to wait on another customer.

Ten minutes later he approached the counter with a leather journal and a newspaper.

"It was a pleasure to meet you. Please accept my sympathies for the loss of your mother."

He tried to forget the beautiful redhead as he walked past the white Congregational Church to the brick academy. Could she be one of his students? She looked way too mature to be a schoolgirl. He climbed the granite steps into the foyer and asked the receptionist to direct him to his classroom.

Mr. Bennett was pleased by this bustling little town by the Saco River, the congenial Miller family, Fryeburg Academy, and his classroom. Now if only his mother and Lily would be pleased.

VI

Tetanus

The next morning the entire family sat down for breakfast in the kitchen.

"Isaac, would you like another cup of coffee?" Lydia asked her bleary-eyed husband who nodded absent mindedly. It had been over eight months since the five of them spent the early morning together.

Charlie took a mouthful of scrambled eggs. "Eggs come from chickens. Eggs are good. Chickens are bad. Horses are good."

Isaac tried to smile at his son, as feelings of despair arose. "I should have been there," he berated himself. "What does everyone have planned today?" he asked pleasantly.

"Summer volunteered to sit at the desk to sign in patients this morning. I am almost caught up with the billing. I can report our root cellar is more than half filled with potatoes, carrots, and beets," Lydia began.

"Beets are bad, very bad," Charlie made a face.

"Do not interrupt your mother," Isaac reprimanded. "I see our patients have been faithful in paying their bills. You can expect bushels of apples and gallons of cider next month."

"At this point I will barter any additional produce with Rachel at the store."

"Mahayla, may I assume you will be spending the day in Nana's garden?"

"There is so much to do, and school begins next week," she complained.

"Will you be taking your brother? We must not have a repeat of yesterday's behavior, Charlie," he warned.

"Chickens are bad."

"I will keep him in the garden with me. It was easier when he was content to nap in the sunshine. He can be good company for Grandpa sometimes. I will try to keep him out of the barn."

"Please do. It is the beginning of harvest and Uncle Eli, Jonathan and the boys have much to do." He rose from the table. "Ladies, thank you for a fine breakfast. Charlie, please do the dishes."

"I can do the dishes. Hayley says I am not stupid."

"I know you are not stupid, Charlie. I have some reading to do before office hours. If you will please excuse me."

"Perhaps you could get some rest?" Lydia suggested with concern.

"I am fine, dear."

George Chase was his first house call that afternoon. "Dr. Miller, I am so relieved to see you," Harriet Chase anxiously greeted him. "I fear he has influenza. He is feverish, achy and is complaining of a severe headache," she explained as she escorted him to the bedroom. Jeremy was seated in a chair by his father's bed. He silently nodded a greeting.

"Well, George, how are you feeling today?" he asked as he placed his leather bag on the bed stand. The patient groaned in response.

"I am going to listen to your heart and lungs," he explained as he reached for his stethoscope. He placed one end of the hollow wooden tube to George's chest and bent over, placing his ear at the other end. "I hear your heart is beating rather rapidly," he stated as he moved the stethoscope. "Your lungs are clear. That is a good sign."

He returned the stethoscope to his bag, and removed his new thermometer, a six -inch glass cylinder filled with mercury. "Let me put this under your tongue for five minutes, and it will record your body temperature."

"I have never seen anything like this," George protested.

"That is because this is a grand improvement over older thermometers. Only ten years ago, they were a foot long and took over twenty minutes to get a reading. Even then, it was not very accurate. Most doctors did not bother to use them."[1]

"How does it work?" Jeremy asked as he stood by the doctor.

"See these lines on the side? Heat will make the mercury rise. I place this end under your father's tongue and remove it five minutes later. Then I read the line where the mercury ends."

"I am not so sure," George shook his head.

"If you prefer, I can take your temperature rectally," Isaac smiled. Jeremy blushed. George opened his mouth. Isaac silently stared at his pocket watch for five minutes before removing the instrument, noting the temperature, wiping it clean with a soft rag, and returning it to its leather case.

"I am going to examine and wash the wound," he explained as he began unwrapping the bandages. "Who wrapped this?" he asked.

"I did, sir," Jeremy answered tentatively.

"Fine job, son." He tried not to reveal his dismay as he observed an infection beginning at the sutures. "Let me wash and rewrap it." The room was silent as Isaac completed the procedure. "George, you have a mild temperature and the beginnings of an infection. How is the pain? Do you need some morphine?"

"My head. I cannot stand this headache."

Isaac took out the glass syringe and the glass bottle of morphine. "This will take the edge off and help you rest. I shall return early evening."

"Is it bad?" George asked anxiously.

"We will know more this evening."

It was still daylight when Isaac returned. Jeremy ran to the carriage to greet him. "Pa has a terrible backache. He says it is unbearable. He needs more morphine!"

Isaac swallowed hard, calmly grabbed his doctor bag as he hopped down from the carriage. "Jeremy could you please give my horse some water?" He did not want the lad to hear the news he had to deliver to his parents.

"How are you feeling, George?" Isaac sat down on the side of the bed and took his patient's pulse.

"Terrible!" he snapped. "My head! My back!"

"Please, Dr. Miller, can you not help him?" Mrs. Chase pleaded.

"Let me get my thermometer," he reached for his bag.
"Get away from me! Get away!" he yelled.

One look at his perspiring patient and the warmth of his hand, told Isaac George's temperature was rising fast. "This will help," he took out the syringe. It took a few minutes before George felt any relief.

"The infection is spreading. This may be a good time to telegraph your sons. I am sure they will be a great help and comfort to you." George had two older sons, Henry a shopkeeper in Boston and Asa, a farmer in Ohio. His third son died in the war.

"Is my Pa going to die?" Jeremy ran into the bedroom.

"That is certainly a possibility. I am still hopeful he will survive. However, he will get worse before he gets better. I think you and your mother will appreciate the extra help with your brothers here. You will be able to get some rest. They can help with the harvest. It may take three or four of you to move him."

"George, Dr. Miller is correct. I would feel so much better if the boys were here," Mrs. Chase agreed.

"Hmmm," George drifted off to sleep.

"That dose should let him sleep through the night. I can stop at the Western Union Office on my way home," Isaac offered. "Both of you should get some sleep."

It was twilight as Isaac entered the home of Dr. D. L. Lamson.[2] In addition to being a highly respected physician, he also ran the telegraph office in a room in his house. FATHER IS DYING STOP COME TO FRYEBURG IMMEDIATELY STOP.

Isaac did not hesitate to ask this more experienced doctor for advice. "Dr. Lamson, my patient has the onset of tetanus. Do you know of any latest studies on its treatment?"

The older man looked at his younger colleague compassionately. "Continue to do what you are doing – keep him comfortable and notify his family," he nodded to the telegraph machine. "You may want to contact Reverend Stone for spiritual support for the family, and James Rogers, the cabinet maker to order a coffin. Sadly, there is nothing more you can do."

"Thank you, Dr. Lamson."

———❋———

Office hours would begin promptly at nine in the morning. "Lydia, I should return before nine. If all goes well," he clarified.

"How is he this morning?" he asked Mrs. Chase as he entered the kitchen.

"He is asleep. Would you like some eggs and coffee?" she offered.

"Thank you. You are most kind." He sat down at the table.

"He refuses to eat or drink anything. He says he cannot swallow."

Isaac gratefully drank his coffee and hoped George's sons would arrive in time.

———❋———

Henry Chase still had the telegram he received twenty-four hours ago folded in his jacket pocket, as the train stopped at the Fryeburg station. He had not been home since his brother's memorial service back in '64 and was uncertain of his next move. "Excuse me, sir," he approached the conductor, "where would I find Dr. Miller's office?" He was well acquainted with

Dr. William Towle and his father the late Dr. Ira Towle but knew nothing about this new doctor.

"The big white house on the corner of Main and Bridge Streets."

"Is that not Senator Miller's house?"

"It was. It is his grandson's house now. He is the doctor."

Henry grabbed his valise and headed toward Main Street. Mahayla answered the front door.

"Is the doctor in?"

"I am sorry, sir. He is out on a call. How may I help you?"

"I am Henry Chase…"

"Dr. Miller is with your father now. Please come in and take a seat. I will borrow my uncle's carriage and take you there," she offered.

However, Lydia would not permit her daughter to traipse through town with a married man. Daniel volunteered to escort Henry to the farm.

Mrs. Chase flung open the front door and ran to the carriage. "Henry, thank God you have come!"

"May I come in as well?" Daniel asked hesitantly.

"Mr. Miller, how kind of you. Yes, of course."

George's eyes lit up as Henry entered the bedroom. He unsuccessfully tried to talk.

"Pa cannot talk. This morning he woke up and could not open his mouth," Jeremy explained.

"Does my father have lock jaw?" he turned to Isaac.

"The proper name is tetanus. But yes, I am afraid he does. When the horse kicked him, it shattered his tibia – his shin bone. Its hoof was covered with dirt and manure and the filth entered his body. I amputated his leg with hopes of stopping any infection from spreading. Your mother and brother have done an outstanding job in cleaning the wound and caring for your father. He could not have received better care.

I am sorry. There is nothing more I can do to stop the infection from taking its course. I promise I will do everything I can to keep him as comfortable as possible."

George grabbed Henry's hand and Jeremy ran out of the room before anyone could see his tears.

"Henry, your father wrote up his will a few days ago. He has accepted his fate. I am so grateful that you are here to spend his last days with him. He thinks the world of you boys," Mrs. Chase struggled to keep her composure. "He would like you to stay and help us harvest the crops and get the firewood. We will rent out the farm in the spring."

"Pa, of course I will stay and help," Henry reassured his father. "Pa, I will stay as long as I am needed."

George nodded and squeezed his son's hand.

The following morning George Chase received a telegram stating his middle son, Asa, would arrive by train on Friday afternoon. Isaac hoped George would still be alive.

---❈---

Jeremy arrived at the train station just as the train pulled to a stop. Asa looked around for a familiar face when he noticed a young man waving. He grabbed his two canvas totes and headed toward the wagon.

"Jeremy, is that you? You are all grown up!" he asked as he threw the totes in the back of the wagon and climbed up to the seat. "Did I make it in time?"

Jeremy nodded. "The doctor is with him now. He only goes home to sleep and to see patients in the morning. Pa mostly sleeps. It is horrible when the morphine begins to wear off."

Asa looked at his young brother with pity. The lad had two days' worth of stubble on his chin and dark circles under his eyes. His hands slightly trembled with exhaustion as he held the reins.

"Henry here?" Jeremy nodded. "How did this happen?"

"Kicked by the horse. Lock jaw."

Asa said nothing for a moment. "You have been with Pa the whole time?"

"Mostly. Ma and I take turns at night."

"Well, Henry and I are here. You get some rest. I am sorry that Ohio is so far away. I should have visited before now."

"You have a family. You are here now. That is all that matters."

———— ❊ ————

The congregation was seated. Just as Reverend Stone began the sermon, the church door opened, and Henry Chase ran up the aisle shouting "Dr. Miller! Come quick! His bones are breaking!"

The church gasped, for most of them knew of the horror that was to follow. Isaac calmly walked down the aisle. Once outside, he quickly limped to his office, grabbed his bags, mounted his horse, and galloped to the Chase farm.

Isaac found the family frantically holding down George's limbs as his muscles violently spasmed. The sound of a large crack filled the room.

"I am sorry. I should have never left last night," Isaac apologized as he opened his bag.

"What just happened?" Asa asked in terror.

"His spine snapped." He took out the all too familiar syringe and a new bottle of morphine. "I will give him as much as I can."

Isaac knew too much morphine would kill him. "Death would be welcomed compared to dying in agony in the next twenty-four hours. No one would ever know. One more injection and it would all be over. No one would ever know," an inner voice tempted. He wiped off the syringe and returned it and the bottle to his bag.

"Dr. Miller, would you like dinner? A neighbor dropped off some stew, bread, pie, and cider."

"Yes, thank you. Do you have any coffee?"

The grieving family ate silently until Jeremy asked, "Will the end be soon?"

"In a few hours. Daybreak the latest."

"Mercy, we do not have a coffin!" Mrs. Chase put down her spoon.

"I took the liberty of speaking with Mr. Rogers," Isaac assured.

"Let us save this conversation for tomorrow," Asa suggested. "Excuse me, I need to take a walk."

"I suggest all of you take a walk. It is not healthy to sit by a death bed for days. I will sit with him." Isaac offered.

He helplessly sat by the bed listening to George's shallow breathing. "You could end this nightmare once and for all," the voice reiterated.

"It will be over soon, George," he whispered and stared out the window.

An oil lamp cast a dim light on the five kitchen chairs circling the bed. Mrs. Chase sat closest to her husband's side. Jeremy was slumped in his chair dozing as Henry and Asa sat silently listening to their father's labored breathing. George moaned and began to stir.

Isaac quickly went to his patient's side. "George, your family is with you," he whispered. George's eyes flew open as he strained to look around the room.

Asa was the first to speak. "Pa, I came from Ohio. I am here." He took his father's hand.

"Pa do not worry. We will take care of everything," Henry assured.

Jeremy awoke, stood at the foot of the bed, and stared into his father's eyes.

George tried to smile before his leg convulsed in a muscle spasm. He groaned loudly.

Isaac filled the syringe and injected the correct dose of morphine. The muscles relaxed and the room filled with the sounds of shallow breathing.

It was daybreak when George Chase took his last breath.

"Is he dead?" Jeremy whispered.

"Yes," Isaac quietly replied. "He was blessed to have his family with him. Your father was a good man. I only regret that I could not save him," he sadly replied as he packed his bag.

Asa walked him out to his horse. "I fear I am just a poor farmer and cannot pay your bill. Please take this as a down payment," he handed Isaac a silver dollar.

"You will need traveling money for your journey home," Isaac protested. "Patients often pay me a combination of cash, produce from their gardens, hay for my horse, merchandise from their stores, or services like cooking or laundry. You sit down with the family and write up a payment plan. I will sign it. It was a pleasure meeting you and your brother. I only regret it was under such difficult circumstances." They shook hands before Isaac saddled his horse and slowly set off for home filled with despair.

VII

Charlie's First Day Back in School

"Did Papa come home last night?" Mahayla asked her mother at the breakfast table.

"I am afraid not," Lydia replied. "Are you girls ready for school?"

"Yes, mam," Summer replied.

"What about Charlie?" Mahayla asked.

"He is not well enough. I fear he may never be well enough."

"I mean who is going to watch Charlie?"

"He and Charlie Doll are sound asleep. When he wakes, we will spend some time together in the office. I will take him for a walk and perhaps visit Grandpa in the afternoon until you girls return from school. Now run along. You do not wish to be late on the first day."

The house was quiet when Charlie awoke two hours later. Where was Mahayla? She would never leave for Grandpa's without him. Then he remembered yesterday they talked about new dresses for the first day of school. They were already at school. "I am late," he mumbled. "Late is bad, very bad." He dressed in his Sunday best, grabbed his wool bag with a slate, *Webster's Blue Backed Speller, Book I of the McGuffey's Readers,* and two pieces of soapstone. He stuffed Charlie Doll in the bag. There was no time for breakfast because he was late. He quietly descended the back staircase, slipped out the back door and ran to the Main Street.

He forgot to look both ways and a horse and wagon swerved to avoid hitting him. "Look where you are going! Idiot!" the driver yelled.

Charlie shook his fist yelling "I am not an idiot! Hayley says I am not stupid. I am not stupid." He muttered, "I am not stupid. I am not stupid," as he ran to the school yard. When he entered the one room schoolhouse, he stopped uncertain as to what to do next. Another boy was sitting in his seat! Miss Warren was writing addition problems on the blackboard.

Students began to whisper, and the teacher turned around, "What is the meaning of this, class?" she asked before she spied Charlie standing in the back. "Why Charlie, what a surprise. Are you feeling better?"

"I am late. Late is bad, very bad," he mumbled. A few students snickered.

"Yes, you are. Please do not let it happen again. Please take a seat," she pointed to an empty space on a bench beside an unfamiliar student.

"This is not my seat. That is my seat!" he pointed to another desk.

"That was your seat last year before you took sick. This is your new seat."

"This is not my seat."

The teacher took him by the arm, led him to the empty seat and pushed him down. "This is your seat. Now take out your slate and soapstone and copy down these figures," she commanded.

"Numbers are good. Numbers are good," he muttered cheerfully for Charlie always excelled in arithmetic. He remembered how to add one-digit numbers, two- digit numbers and even to carry over the tens. "Numbers are good. Chickens are bad. Numbers are good."

"Chickens are good. Numbers are bad," his seatmate hissed. "Chickens are good. Numbers are bad."

Charlie stood up and yelled, "No! Numbers are good. Chickens are bad."

The teacher swiftly walked over to Charlie's desk. "Charlie, what has gotten into you? You know better than that. Now go stand in the corner."

"Yes, mam." A repentant Charlie stood in the corner whispering "Numbers are good. Chickens are bad."

Miss Warren checked the arithmetic on Charlie's slate. "Charlie, if you are ready to behave yourself, you may return to your seat. I see you did not forget your addition while you were sick. Now try some subtraction while I work with the younger students."

He was concentrating on his subtraction trying to ignore the boy behind him poking him in the back. "Numbers are good," he whispered. He had to think how to borrow from the tens' column. He felt the frustration rising as he wanted to yell at the boy behind him to stop. He could not concentrate. He knew his answer was wrong as he shut his eyes for a moment.

As the youngest students were reciting the alphabet, Miss Warren could not hear the boys taunting him, "Chickens are good. Chickens are good."

Charlie ignored them, but he knew his subtraction answers were wrong.

"When did this become a school for idiots and imbeciles?" one boy snickered.

"I am not an idiot!" he stood up and screamed. "I am not stupid! Hayley says I am not stupid!"

"Idiot!" the boy smirked.

Charlie smashed his slate over the student's head. The boy screamed in pain as blood ran down the side of his face.

"I am not stupid!"

"Benjamin Charles Miller! Go stand in the corner immediately!" commanded Miss Warren as she took a cotton handkerchief from her sleeve and began to dab at the wailing boy's wound.

"I am not an idiot!" he screamed as he grabbed his school bag and ran out the door. "Blood is bad, very bad." He did not know where to go. He knew he would be in trouble if he went home. Perhaps he would run to see Grandpa. But the chickens might be out. He took Charlie Doll out of the bag and ran to find a safe place where there would be no chickens and no mean boys calling him names.

※

Isaac found two patients waiting for him in the office when he arrived. "May I get you a cup of coffee?" Lydia offered.

"I would be most appreciative," he replied glumly.

She need not ask about Mr. Chase, for Isaac's eyes told the story. "The girls are at the Academy and Charlie is still asleep. Perhaps you can get some rest this afternoon."

"I will be with you as soon as I have my coffee," he addressed the waiting room.

Suddenly the front door opened with an older student escorting a sobbing, young boy holding a bloody handkerchief to his head.

"What happened?" Isaac asked gently.

"Charlie smashed his slate over his head," the older boy explained.

"Charlie who?" Lydia asked in disbelief.

"Charlie Miller."

"Your son hit me," the patient accused.

"That is impossible. He is upstairs sleeping." A look of horror crossed her face as she ran upstairs calling "Charlie! Charlie!" She found an unmade bed, his night clothes strewn on the floor, Charlie Doll and his school bag missing. She frantically searched all the bedrooms calling "Charlie!" before returning to the office.

Isaac was carefully washing the wound. "I know blood can be scary. There are no pieces of slate in the wound, and I do not believe you need stitches. Press this clean cloth against your head for a few minutes until the bleeding stops. Then I will bandage it and take you home. You will have a headache for a day or two.

Now explain to me how this happened."

"Charlie was sitting in front of me, and we were doing arithmetic. He kept saying chickens were bad. Some of the boys were teasing him."

Lydia's heart sank.

"Why did he hit you? Were you teasing him?"

"Yes, sir."

"What did you say to him?" Isaac tried to sound calm as he felt anger rising.

"I called him an idiot. He hit me over the head and started yelling he was not stupid."

"Do you know that Charlie almost died of rheumatic fever last year?"

"Yes, sir."

"Do you think it is kind to call a sick child a mean name?"

"No, sir."

"Charlie was wrong to hit you. He is not ready to go back to school. You were wrong to call him a name. Perhaps you will think twice before you call someone names."

"Dr. Miller, I can walk him home. You have sick people waiting for you," the older student offered. That was better than going back to school right away.

"Thank you, young man."

"Dr. Miller, I am sorry that Charlie got sick. I hope he gets better," the older boy offered his sincere regrets.

"Thank you, I do too." He finished bandaging the wound.

"I can help you find Charlie," he offered.

"Please take our patient home and return to school. Charlie could not have gone far. He tires easily."

The two boys left. "Lydia, I have two more patients. Perhaps you can check the farm to see if he is visiting with my father and bring him home."

"No, I have not seen Charlie," Julia explained as she welcomed Lydia into the kitchen. She went to the front parlor, "Father Miller, is Charlie with you?"

"No. I have not seen him since church yesterday."

"I am sure he has not gone far. You know he tires easily," Lydia repeated Isaac's reassuring words.

"I will check the barn to see if Eli or Jonathan have seen him," Julia offered. She returned shaking her head.

"He may have stopped by to visit Danny. I will check there," Lydia hoped she sounded optimistic.

"I will join you," Julia offered.

Eli entered the room. "I will get the wagon and go search for him. He is probably exhausted and will need a ride home."

Emily opened the kitchen door. "Lydia, Julia what a surprise. Let me make some tea," she offered.

"We cannot stay. Charlie is missing. I hoped he stopped by here."

Daniel entered the kitchen. "Did someone say Charlie is missing?"

Lydia's tears slid down her cheeks as she explained, "This is all my fault. I thought he was sleeping when I went to the office. I did not see him when he went off to school. He was involved in an altercation with another student and ran out of the school. No one knows where he went. I should have…"

"Have a cup of tea with Emily and then return home. Charlie may already be there. Julia and I will go to the general store to see if Charlie is there. Or perhaps Rachel or someone saw him walk by," Daniel offered as he grabbed his hat and headed out the door.

"Did I see Charlie? No. Why? Is he missing?" Rachel asked in alarm. "Peter, did you see Charlie?" she called to her husband who was working in the back of the store.

"I am going to look for him," she declared as she took off her apron and put on her bonnet.

"I will ask every customer who comes in, if they have seen him," Peter offered. "Did someone check the cemetery? It is right behind the school, and it is a great place to hide."

"I will go there first," Rachel announced.

"I will check the Academy to see if he went looking for Mahayla," Daniel stated.

"I will stop in every store and the Oxford House. Even if he did not stop in, people may have seen him," Julia explained.

Julia spied John Smith tending his horses. "Mr. Smith, have you seen my nephew, Charlie? He ran away from school, and he is missing.

"I have not. You continue down Main Street, and I will canvass the side streets," he volunteered.

Next, she stopped in Shirley & Lewis store on the corner of Main Street and Portland Street. Alonzo Lewis greeted her, "Good morning, Mrs. Miller, how may I help you?"

"Have you seen my nephew, Charlie. He ran away from school."

"Allow me to look for him. I will continue looking on this side of the street while you search across the street. I will be out for a while," he called to his business partner.

By two o'clock that afternoon half the village was out searching for him.

---❋---

Emerson Bennett was quite pleased with his students on this first day of school. They were bright and inquisitive, not at all the country rubes his acquaintances back in Concord warned him about. He decided to enjoy the early autumn sunshine and leisurely walk back to his room. Stepping down the granite steps he found the village in an uproar, and Mahayla Miller standing in the road weeping. Next to her stood the mysterious, beautiful redhead.

"Miss Miller," he approached Mahayla, "what is wrong? May I be of assistance?" he asked kindly.

"Our brother is missing," Summer answered.

The Fryeburg Chronicles Book VI

"Mr. Bennett, unbeknownst to us, Charlie left for school. The students were mean to him, and he ran off. He has been missing for hours," Mahayla explained.

It was only then did he realize the lovely young woman he admired from afar was Summer Miller, Mahayla's older sister.

"Please let me walk you home. Your mother must be frantic and would be comforted by your presence. Where do you think he would be? I will go search," he offered.

"People have already looked where I thought he might be. Uncle Eli organized a group of men to paddle down the Saco just in case…"

Reverend Stone, who was returning from a visit with the Chase family, pulled up in his carriage. "Mahayla, What is wrong?"

"Charlie has been missing for hours. I have offered to walk them home," Mr. Bennett explained.

"He cannot have gone far. He gets exhausted walking to church Sunday mornings," the pastor observed.

"Reverend, is the church building unlocked?" Mr. Bennett asked.

"As a matter of fact, it is."

The instructor ran down Main Street with Mahayla, Summer, and the good pastor, following from a distance.

He ran up the granite steps panting as he entered the building. He heard a voice from the front of the sanctuary. "I am not stupid! Hayley says I am not stupid."

Mr. Lewis sat with Charlie in the front pew consoling him. "Everyone knows you are not stupid. You have been seriously ill. You are not ready to go to school. You must continue your recovery."

Mr. Bennett quietly walked to the front. "Charlie Miller, Mahayla is crying. She is afraid you are lost."

"I am not lost. I am right here, see. Tell Hayley not to cry."

"Let us go find Hayley and you can show her that you are not lost," Mr. Lewis stretched out his hand. Charlie tentatively took his hand and the three of them exited the church and walked up Main Street.

"Charlie!" Mahayla ran and greeted him with open arms.

"Do not cry. I am not lost. I am here. School is bad, very bad."

"Mr. Bennett, thank you for finding our brother," Summer said softly. "We must have you to Sunday dinner some time."

"This gentleman found him first." He nodded at Mr. Lewis.

"Mr. Lewis, thank you for searching for him," Mahayla said.

"Now, may I escort all three of you home?" Mr. Bennett offered.

"Mama, I am not lost. I am here," Charlie greeted his mother as he entered the kitchen.

"I have been worried sick over you!" she scolded.

"Mr. Bennett and Mr. Lewis found him in church," Summer explained.

"Thank you, sir. May I impose upon you?"

"Why of course."

"Could you please go to the farm and tell my father-in-law you have found Charlie. I fear he is having one of his spells and has taken to his bed. First, he lost his wife and today he thought he lost another grandson. Dr. Miller is searching for him on the river with his brother."

"Yes, Mam. I am on my way."

Word soon passed through the village that Emerson Bennett, the new instructor at the Academy, found the missing boy hiding in the church. Half the folks thank the Lord for finding the child and bringing him home to his distraught parents. The other half shook their heads in dismay.

The clock on the mantle in Isaac's office struck ten when Lydia entered. "He and Charlie Doll are finally asleep." She collapsed in the nearby chair, "This is all my fault. I thought he was sleeping. I never heard him leave the house."

Isaac got up from his desk, sat beside his wife, and reassured her, "This is most certainly not your fault. You and the girls have done an extraordinary job in caring for him. For months I hoped and prayed our dear son would make a full recovery. I think it is time for us to accept this is Charlie's new life and adapt to it.

Today could have easily ended in a tragedy. If Charlie had hit him in the face, that poor child could have lost his sight in one eye. If Charlie was stronger and had hit him harder, he could have killed him.

If we cannot control him now, what will he be like ten years from now? We cannot expect Summer and Mahayla to devote their lives to their brother's care. I wish for them to marry and raise families of their own. What will Charlie be like thirty or forty years from now? His grandfather, aunt and uncles will all be dead, and we shall be too old to care for him. That is why we need to plan for his care now and not wait for a tragedy."

Lydia looked up. "What are you saying?"

"I am saying that there are schools for people like Charlie. I have written letters to the Elm Hill Private School and Home for the Education of the Feeble Minded in Barre, Massachusetts and the Massachusetts School for Idiots and Feeble Minded in Waverly, Massachusetts. We can visit each institution before we make our decision."

Lydia quietly wept for the loss of her Charlie, the healthy and vibrant eight-year-old who never returned to her.

Mahayla who was standing at the top of the stairs heard every word.

VIII

Charlie's New School

Mahayla quietly descended the back staircase, grabbed her shawl, and left through the kitchen before running to her grandfather's farm. As Mr. Bennett sat at his desk penning a letter to Lily, he spied Mahayla running by the light of the full moon and pounding on the back door of the farm next door.

Eli opened the door. "Mahayla, what is wrong?"

"Uncle Eli, Papa is going to send Charlie to a school for idiots and the feeble minded in Massachusetts. Grandpa must stop him!"

Jacob exited his first-floor bedroom and entered the kitchen. "What is all this yelling?"

"Grandpa, Papa wants to send Charlie away to a school for idiots. It is not Charlie's fault he is the way he is."

"Over my dead body! I lost two grandsons, and I will not lose a third. Elijah, hitch the wagon for me. I must talk some sense into that son of mine."

"I will go with you, Pa," Eli offered.

"Should we get Uncle Danny?" Mahayla asked.

"No. Get your aunt Rachel."

Mr. Bennett tentatively knocked on the open door to the family parlor where Daniel was reading.

"Please excuse me for intruding, sir."

"Not at all. Please come in for I would like to hear about your first day of school. With all the excitement today, I had forgotten to ask you about it at dinner."

"We shall save that discussion for tomorrow. While sitting at my desk, I spied Mahayla run to the farm, and now the three of them are headed back to Dr. Miller's. Please forgive me if I have overstepped my boundaries, but I fear something is wrong and you may want to learn about it."

"Of course. Thank you, Mr. Bennett. I shall take a walk over there."

Daniel found Eli, his father, and his sister in Isaac's office talking excitedly.

"You know when David returned from the war, he wasn't the same son I had before. I would give everything I own to get him back, even with all his problems. What kind of father would give up his only son?" Eli demanded.

"Elijah James, that is enough," Jacob warned his eldest. "Isaac, why would you want to do such a thing?"

"Charlie could have killed that boy today. If I cannot control him when he is nine years old, what will happen when he is twenty or forty? Will he end up in jail? I have been told that Charlie is not welcomed at school. What will he do all day? What will he do as an adult? Will he ever have a job and support himself? Will he marry and have a family?"

"He has a family," Rachel firmly stated. "He can work at the store stocking shelves. He is very good in math: he can make change."

"He can spend the mornings with me," Daniel offered. "I will teach him to read and read books to him. I will teach him how to care for my horse and drive a wagon. He can help me deliver food to the sick and needy in our congregation. I will teach him from the Bible."

Mahayla entered the room. "When I return home from school, I can take him to the herb garden and show him how to weed and water the plants, pick, and dry them. Nana would not want Charlie sent away."

"When he is at the farm, I will tell him stories about the family," Jacob added.

"Any child will get into mischief if he is left to his own devices. Children need structure and boundaries. The matter has been settled," Rachel declared. "All of us will spend part of the day with Charlie."

"I am not an idiot!" Charlie stood in the waiting room dressed in his night shirt and holding Charlie Doll. "I am not stupid. Hayley says I am not stupid. I do not want to go to school. The boys are mean, very mean."

"You do not have to go to school," Isaac sadly relented.

"Tomorrow morning you will come to my house." Daniel explained.

"After lunch you will work in the store," Rachel continued.

"I will pick you up after school, and we will work in the garden until supper."

"It has been a very long day, and we are all exhausted. Charlie, go to bed without a fuss. We will try this new schedule for a month and then I will reevaluate the situation," he declared as he put the letters in his desk's top drawer. "I appreciate everyone's concern," he stood up at his desk. "Good night," he dismissed his family as he left the office and went upstairs.

"He is exhausted," Lydia explained. "George Chase died this morning. He needs a good night's sleep. Thank you for coming over. Your help means a lot to me – to both of us."

"Poor Jeremy," Mahayla thought. "That is why he was not in school today." She ran upstairs to her room, closed the door, and sobbed. It had been an overwhelming day.

Wordlessly, the rest of the family returned to their homes.

The next morning Daniel found Isaac in his office peering into his microscope.

"We found a vaccine for smallpox. Can we not find one for tetanus?" he muttered to himself.

"Perhaps we will someday."

Isaac looked up startled. "I did not hear you arrive. You are early. Charlie is not up yet. Lydia thought it best for him to sleep in."

"I came early to talk to you."

"You are not going to quote Bible verses to me, are you?" he accused.

"I came to tell you I am sorry."

"For what?"

"For all that you have experienced these past few years. I know that Darian's death was very difficult for you. I am sorry that I was so involved in my own grief, I was not very helpful. You were never the same after David's death."

Isaac closed his eyes and shuddered at the memory of his nephew's body hanging from the barn rafters.

"It was not an accident, was it?"

For a moment Isaac was tempted to reveal the secret – all the secrets that were haunting him. He said nothing.

"I am sorry that I was so busy helping Pa and Eli care for Ma, I did not help you care for Charlie. I am sorry that I did not stand up to Eli last night. He had no right to say what he did."

"Eli has not been the same since David's death. He could not accept David's problems after the war, and after his death, Eli realized what he lost. He was right. I panicked. Those schools should be the last resort, not my first option. I need to accept the new Charlie and plan accordingly."

"It is more than Charlie that is hurting you. I can see it."

Isaac turned to his brother. What good would it do to break his promise and reveal the secrets he had kept for years? "George Chase was my first patient with tetanus. I hope I never have another one. It was the most gruesome death I have ever witnessed, and I have witnessed many on the battlefield. I was tempted to give him an overdose of morphine and end it sooner. What kind of doctor would think of such a thing?"

"An exhausted one. An overly burdened one. When was the last time you slept?"

"A few hours ago."

"No. I mean, when was the last time you spent the night sleeping? Days? Weeks? Months?"

"Uncle!" Charlie burst into the office still dressed in his nightshirt. "Charlie Doll and I are very excited to spend the morning with you. I promised Mama that I would be on my best behavior, and I will not hit anyone today."

"Good morning, Charlie," Emily greeted as she was washing the breakfast dishes. "Are you ready for school today?"

"Yes. Charlie Doll and I have our books. I do not have my slate. I broke it in school. I was angry, very angry and I broke it. That was a sin."

"Did your parents tell you that?" Daniel asked.

"No."

"Did your sisters tell you that?" Emily suggested.

"The Bible told me that. I am bad, very bad," he lamented.

"The Bible says we are all sinners. Jesus came to the world to save sinners," Daniel kindly explained. "We do not earn our way to heaven by trying to be good."

"That is good news. Very good news," Charlie gave a sigh of relief.

"Emily, we will be in the front parlor. Today we will begin reading Proverbs."

"I am not a good reader. Numbers are good, but reading is bad."

"I will do the reading and you will do the listening. It is important to learn to listen. You cannot learn if you do not listen."

"Listening is good, very good."

The two of them sat on the settee with Charlie Doll in the middle. Daniel opened the large leather-bound Bible. "This belonged to my great grandfather James, who was a minister in Boston, before he moved to Fryeburg. It is over one hundred years old," he opened the front cover. "See, every Miller who was born is listed right here." He pointed to a name on the list. "This says Benjamin Charles Miller."

"My name is in the Bible," he beamed.

"Yes, it is because you are a child of Isaac Miller and a child of God. Today we are going to read from Proverbs."

"King Solomon wrote Proverbs. He was a smart king. He was very smart. I listen in church sometimes."

Daniel read Proverbs 1:7 "'The fear of the Lord is the beginning of knowledge; fools despise wisdom and instruction.' Wisdom is a gift from God. It is the ability to understand what the Lord wants you to understand."

"Do I have to know how to read first?"

"No. In fact there are people who read many books and they have no wisdom."

"That is good, very good to know. I do not want to be a fool. I want to be wise, very wise."

---❋---

After lunch Daniel escorted Charlie to Evans General Store. Peter Evans greeted his young nephew. "Just in time. I need your help at the railroad station."

Charlie hesitated. "Charlie Doll does not like trains. They are very big and very, very loud."

"Would Charlie Doll like to stay here with Aunt Rachel?"

"Will there be chickens at the train station?"

"I have never seen one chicken at the train station in all these years," Peter reported.

"Will you be taking your horse?" Charlie asked.

"Absolutely. I need him to pull the wagon."

"Horses are good."

"Horses are good. Some people are afraid of horses."

"I am not afraid of horses. Horses are good."

"Trains are good. They are noisy and dirty, but they make life much easier. Before the train, I had to take my horse and wagon in all kinds of weather to Portland. I would load up my wagon. Sometimes I spent the night there and spent the next day riding home. I would be away from the store for two days. Now I can pick up my merchandise and return in less than an hour. Do you know you can take a train clear across the country?"

"I guess trains are good."

❋

"Charlie, you are a hard worker, We stocked all the merchandise on the shelves," Peter complimented. What he did not mention was he could have done it in half the time.

"Charlie Doll helped too," he pointed to the doll sitting on the counter.

"Can you watch the store while I bring the crates to the back room?"

As Peter left, two young men entered, nudging each other, and laughing. "Do you have any dolls for sale?" they pointed at Charlie Doll.

"No, sir. This doll is not for sale. He works here."

The men laughed louder. "I would like to buy a pound of soap."

Charlie nervously looked around for his aunt or uncle. "Yes, sir." He cut a pre-marked rectangle of soap and measured it on the scale just to be certain. "That is eight cents please,"

The customer handed him a dime. Charlie returned two pennies in change.

"You made a mistake. Are you trying to cheat me?" the taller man accused. "You owe me a quarter!"

"Numbers are good. One dime equals ten pennies. The soap cost eight pennies. Ten minus eight is two. Everybody knows that. A quarter is twenty-five pennies, not two pennies. Everybody knows that!"

The second man laughed. "Yeah, Tom, everybody knows that. Even the village idiot. Leave the poor boy alone."

"I am not stupid. Hayley says I am not stupid."

Aunt Rachel entered with a swishing of petticoats, and the stomping of leather soles on the wooden floor. "Gentleman, I do not want or need your business. If you dare to show your faces here again, I will throw you out."

The taller man smirked. "Come on, Tom, just leave."

"Do you think I am afraid of an idiot and an old lady!"

"Is there a problem here?" Reverend Stone entered with a half dozen ladies from the Missionary Society.

"He is a big sinner," Charlie pointed to the taller man. "A very big sinner. I sold him a pound of soap for eight cents and gave him two pennies back from his dime. He says I owe him a quarter. Numbers are good."

"Well, I heard what you said young man," Mrs. Weston fearlessly approached him. "I have a mind to wash out your mouth with that soap!" she grabbed the package from him.

Tom took a step back as Mrs. Bradley stuck out her cane. He crashed to the floor.

"You two need to show some respect for your elders!" Mrs. Walker wagged her finger in his face as he was rising to his feet.

"Are you boys from Fryeburg?" the pastor asked.

"No. We are just passing through. Don't want no trouble."

"Gentlemen, let me escort you to the town line," Reverend Stone offered. "The Bible has much to say about sinners…"

The two men ran out the door without their soap or two pennies.

———✻———

Summer and Mahayla dropped by to pick up Charlie. "How was your first day of… Where is Charlie?" Mahayla asked her aunt. She pointed upstairs." He locked himself in our bedroom." Rachel described the incident.

Mahayla ran upstairs and knocked on the locked door.

"I am not stupid. Hayley says I am not stupid," the sobbing child repeated.

"Charlie, you are not stupid. Did Mrs. Bradley really trip him with her cane? I wish I could have seen that."

"The door opened. That man was a big sinner. I did not hit him, but I wanted to."

"I am proud of you, Charlie. Nana's garden is waiting for me, and Grandpa is waiting for you.

Charlie refused to enter his grandfather's house to visit and sat on the grass near the garden clutching Charlie Doll. "I would never sell you or send you away to school for bad dolls," he whispered. "I am not an idiot. I am not an idiot."

"You are not an idiot. You are a blessing!" Jacob corrected. "Come sit with me on the bench by the river. We need to talk man to man." At first the two of them simply stared at the Saco River. Jacob cleared his throat. "I lost two grandsons."

"Where did they go?"

"They both died."

"Dying is bad, very bad."

"Uncle Danny and Aunt Emily did not have any children of their own. Then one day a boy, about your age, came to Fryeburg from a faraway country named Ireland."

"Did his parents miss him?"

"No. His parents, grandparents, brothers and sisters all died because they did not have enough food to eat."

Charlie started crying. "That is sad, very, very, very sad."

"His name was Darian, and he was your father's best friend. They did everything together. Darian went to live with Uncle Danny and Aunt Emily, and they loved him just as if he was their son. I loved him just like my grandson. They both fought in the war. One day your father was seriously wounded and would have died on the battlefield. But Darian left his post and carried him a long way to a doctor."

"The doctor cut off his leg, you know."

"I know. But your father would have died if the doctor had not cut off his leg."

"Papa cut off Mr. Chase's leg and he died," Charlie pointed out.

"Your father came close to dying. Darian wrote a letter to Uncle Danny asking him to go to the town of Gettysburg to find him and give him food and medicine. It was dangerous for him to go into town alone without the other soldiers. But he knew that your father would die without the extra food and medicine. On his way back to the battlefield, he was captured by the enemy and thrown into a prison camp. He died there two years later. Your father never recovered from that.

Uncle Eli had a son named David. In fact, you look quite a bit like him when he was your age."

"Did he die in the war too?"

"He was hurt and lost in the war. When he returned home, he found life hard. He died in an accident in the barn. Both my grandsons were gone. Then a few years later the Good Lord gave me one more grandson and I knew he was a blessing from above. We named him Benjamin Miller, after my father. My father was Benjamin James, and my grandson is Benjamin Charles."

"That's me! I am a blessing?"

"Yes, you are."

"I am not an idiot. I am a blessing."

IX

The Accident

Mr. Bennett shivered under the blankets as he listened to the freezing rain and winds rattle the windows, one mid- November morning. He could procrastinate no longer, for he heard the boys on the second floor getting out of bed. He was the last one to the dining room as Daniel began reading from Proverbs.

The opening and slamming of the back door interrupted Daniel. Dr. Miller poked his head in, "Danny, may I please have a word?"

Danny and Emily found Isaac and Charlie in the kitchen. "Mama says I can eat breakfast with you today."

"Of course, you may. Help me get an extra bowl," she invited.

"Aunt Harriet is dying again today. She insists she must speak to Grandpa," Charlie blurted.

"Charlie, you should not listen to grownups when they are speaking," Isaac scolded.

"Yesterday, you told me to listen when you are talking to me. Grownups are hard to understand, very hard."

"You must be hungry. Follow me," Emily invited as she tried not to laugh.

Isaac turned to his brother. "Aunt Harriet says she must talk to Pa before it is too late. I am on my way now. Could you take Pa in your carriage? I don't want him to ride in Eli's open wagon in this weather."

✼

A group of nieces and nephews surrounded the elderly woman's bed. "Aunt Harriet, it is your nephew, Isaac."

She slowly opened her eyes. "I did not ask for you! You better not charge me for a house call! Where is your father?" she demanded.

"Danny and Pa are on their way."

"I must give him a message from Katie before I die," she closed her eyes and drifted off to sleep.

Thirty minutes later Jacob and Danny arrived, cold, wet, and shivering. "She wants to speak to you, Pa," Isaac greeted him by the door and helped him take off his damp, wool coat.

"Uncle Jacob, let me hang this by the woodstove to dry and make you a cup of coffee," one of his nieces offered as Isaac led his father into the crowded bedroom.

He sat by the side of the bed and took his sister-in-law's hand. "Harriet, I have come to say goodbye. You know you were Kate's favorite sister. She loved you very much."

She slowly opened her eyes and turned to Jacob. "Of course, she did. I was the favorite of the family! My sister truly loved you."

"I know. I did not deserve such a wonderful wife. I miss her every waking moment."

"She found the letter forty years ago. She knew and she did not love you any less. She made me promise to tell you after she was gone. So there, I told you and I can die in peace."

Jacob silently stared at the floor as the relatives looked at one another in bewilderment.

Isaac abruptly changed the subject. "Danny is here. Would you like to pray with him?"

"Heavens no! Cannot an old woman die in peace?"

Daniel said nothing and silently prayed in the corner. The room grew quiet as Jacob sat silently holding Harriet's hand.

———— ❈ ————

Emily was reading to Charlie by the warmth of the woodstove in the front parlor when a loud crash and shattering of glass interrupted them. "Gracious! What was that?" Emily jumped up with a start.

"I think a branch of the old oak tree broke off and smashed the third story window," Charlie calmly stated. "Uncle Eli can fix it. He can fix anything. Can we keep reading?"

"I am going outside to investigate. Wait for me here," she instructed.

Charlie sat staring at the book. "Numbers are good. Words are hard, very hard." He looked at the clock with the Roman numerals. Fifteen minutes had passed, and Aunt Emily did not return. "This is bad, very bad!" he got up, ran to the kitchen, and opened the door. Aunt Emily was lying at the bottom of the stairs! "Aunt Emily! Aunt Emily!" he yelled. "This is bad, very bad," he whispered as he grasped the rail and carefully climbed down the icy steps. "Aunt Emily! It is Charlie. Do not be scared.

I am going to get Uncle Eli. He will help us." He ran down the road to the large farmhouse slipping and falling several times. Each time he pulled himself up and ran faster. "Uncle! Uncle!" he screamed as he ran into his grandfather's barn."

"Charlie, what are you doing out in this weather? Where is your coat?" Eli asked.

"Aunt Emily fell down the stairs. She cannot talk or move. This is bad!"

"Jonathan, get the wagon," he instructed before running into the house. "Julia! Julia! Get Becky and come with us to Danny's house. Emily has fallen!"

"Mercy! How do you know?"

"Charlie ran all the way here to tell us." The women grabbed their cloaks and winter bonnets and climbed into the waiting wagon.

"Charlie, where is your coat?" Julia scolded.

"Aunt Emily needs a doctor. Papa is at Aunt Harriet's house. She is hurt. We must get Papa!"

"We will get Aunt Emily in the house and Jonathan will get your father. In the meantime, I will see if Dr. Towle is home. It will be all right," Eli tried to reassure his nephew. "You were brave to run to the farm all by yourself. Your father and Uncle Danny will be proud of you." He stopped the wagon by the side of the house. Charlie jumped out first.

"She is by the kitchen steps." The rest of the family slowly made their way across the treacherous ice. Eli stopped at the sight of his sister-in-law crumpled on the ground. "She may have broken bones. Jonathan, help me pick her up. Easy now."

"We need Aunt Rachel. She will know what to do." Charlie half slid and half ran down the road, past his house and up the main street. "Aunt Rachel!" he screamed. The store was empty of customers, and Rachel came running downstairs from their apartment. "Aunt Emily fell on the ice. Uncle Eli and Jonathan are trying to pick her up. Papa and Uncle Danny are at Aunt Harriet's house. This is bad, very bad."

"Charlie where is your coat?" but he was already out the door. Reverend Stone heard the pounding on the front door of the parsonage. "Charlie Miller, what are you doing out in this weather without a coat?" he scolded. "Aunt Emily fell on the ice and is hurt very bad. Uncle Eli and Aunt Julia are there. She needs a doctor and Papa and Uncle Danny are at Aunt Harriet's house. Uncle Danny is not home. Who is going to pray for her? You must come now!

I am tired. I am very, very tired." He collapsed on the floor.

Jonathan knocked once at the Wiley's front door.

"I need to speak to Isaac and Daniel. There has been an accident."

By the time Daniel and Isaac arrived, the family had carefully carried Emily inside and gently placed her on the bed. Daniel ran to his wife's side. "Emily, can you hear me?" she groaned loudly and opened her eyes. Isaac entered the bedroom carrying both of his black bags.

"I need to examine my patient. You may shut the door on your way out," he instructed the family.

"I hate it when he uses his doctor tone of voice with us," Eli grumbled as the family assembled in the dining room.

"At the moment Emily is his patient, not his sister-in-law," Julia gently reminded.

"All we can do is wait," Rachel sighed.

"You are wrong. We can pray," Daniel whispered.

Mr. Bennett glanced out the classroom window as he dismissed the last class of the day. He was grateful that it had stopped raining and planned to leave immediately for home. Yesterday he had lost track of time correcting papers and had arrived late for supper. He was setting a poor example for his young scholars and was determined to arrive early and help set the tables.

"Mr. Bennett, you are leaving early," Mahayla greeted him at the bottom of the granite steps. She and Summer were walking arm and arm to help keep their balance as they slowly walked across patches of ice.

"I was late for supper last night," he confessed, "and I do not intend to do so today. May I have the pleasure of escorting you home?"

"I fell twice this morning walking to school. You may need to pick me up," Mahayla laughed. Summer looked mortified at her sister. This was no way for a lady to address a gentleman, and certainly not one of their teachers!

The trio made it safely to Dr. Miller's front door. "Have a good evening, ladies," Mr. Bennett tipped his hat.

"The same to you, sir," Summer replied. Once indoors, she scolded her younger sister, "You are simply impossible!"

Mr. Bennett counted four carriages and wagons parked on the side of the road as he approached the front door. "Mr. and Mrs. Miller must be entertaining," he assumed. Two of his students anxiously greeted him and silently motioned for him to enter the visitors' front parlor. "There has been an accident. Mrs. Miller fell on the ice this morning. Dr. Miller is talking to the family in the dining room."

"She has broken both her tibia and femur," Isaac explained to his siblings.

"What does that mean?" Rachel demanded.

"She has broken her left leg in two places – her lower leg and upper leg. That I know for certain. I can only assume she broke each bone on a different step as she fell. She has either fractured or broken her left hip and several ribs. I set her broken leg."

"Will you need to amputate?" Daniel asked.

"Oh no, not at all. It is nothing like Mr. Chase's shattered leg," he reassured his brother. "I gave her a shot of morphine. She will be in excruciating pain when she wakes up. I will keep her sedated. I set the leg the best I know how. The hip and ribs need weeks if not months of bedrest to heal. We need to wait and see."

"What do you mean wait and see?" Rachel asked.

"To see if she will be able to walk again."

Mr. Bennett quietly rapped on the door. "Please forgive me. Sir, we are so sorry to hear about Mrs. Miller's accident. I will be taking the boys to the Oxford House for supper tonight and supervising them with their studies upstairs. We will endeavor to not disturb you this evening."

"Yes, supper. Yes, the boys. I have forgotten about them," Daniel stated in a daze. "Thank you, Mr. Bennett."

❈

The normally busy dining room at the Oxford House was nearly empty when the five boys and their chaperone arrived. "Welcome," Asa Pike, the owner of the hotel warmly greeted. "You are hearty souls to brave the icy roads. Follow me, please." He pushed two tables together.

After reading the menu several times followed by much discussion and debate, Mr. Bennett ordered a bowl of stew, a loaf of bread and an apple tart for everyone.

Once the food arrived, the boys turned to him, "Mr. Miller always says grace and an evening's benediction at bedtime."

He felt his cheeks turning red. He had never prayed aloud in his entire life. Frankly he could not remember praying at all. He awkwardly mumbled some words which vaguely sounded like one of Mr. Miller's prayers and they began to eat. "Gentleman, Mrs. Miller has been seriously injured and will be bedridden for weeks. Tomorrow morning, we will all rise early and make our own oatmeal and tea. After school I will borrow the wagon from the farm and take you to your homes for the weekend."

"Will we be able to return Sunday night?"

"I do not know the answer to that question. Let us enjoy this meal and return before it grows late. We have studying to do before bed."

The boys relished relaying their childhood adventures of hunting and fishing with their fathers, canoeing down the Saco River, delivering a breeched foal, shingling roofs, tapping maple trees, and harvesting ice. They often referred to school as "book learning". It was apparent that the "important learning" occurred in real life. Mr. Bennett was amazed by the array of experiences which he never had. He envied them.

"The ice man always delivered our ice. I have never observed men harvesting ice," Mr. Bennett confessed.

One boy offered, "We will take you to the pond this winter and show you how it is done."

"What are the winters like in Maine? How much snow falls?"

The boys laughed. "You will see for yourself."

Summer ran into Emily's kitchen calling, "Papa! You must come home!"

Rachel quickly entered, "Shh. What is so important, that cannot wait until morning?"

"Charlie is sick. He is burning up with a fever and delirious. He thinks Charlie Doll is a chicken. Mahayla and Mama are frantic!" The rest of the family and Reverend Stone entered the kitchen.

"I knew he would get sick when he ran all the way to the store without his coat," Rachel declared.

"He also ran to the farm to get us," Julia added.

"He ran all the way to the parsonage," the pastor declared.

Daniel leaned against the wall. "That dear boy risked his health to save his aunt."

Another wagon pulled up and Jacob carefully climbed the back steps and entered the kitchen. Eli greeted him. "Pa, I am so sorry about Aunt Harriet."

"Nonsense. When I left, she was eating boiled ham and potatoes. She will outlive us all. How is Emily?"

"She has a long road to recovery," Isaac tersely answered as he put on his coat. "Excuse me, I need to return home."

Rachel and Julia decided to spend the night. Eli would return to the farm with Jacob. The boys quietly entered the front door and went upstairs. No one knew what the morning would bring.

The Accident

Jeremy listened to the clock in the parlor chime ten. He had milked the cow and collected the eggs hours ago. The farm seemed desolate since his brothers left. As he sat at the kitchen staring at his unopened schoolbooks. The sound of an approaching carriage broke the silence.

"Who could that be?" Mrs. Chase uttered as she put down her sewing and headed to the front door. "Mahayla, come warm yourself by the cookstove while I make us a pot of tea. Please tell me what is troubling you, dear."

Jeremy immediately stood up. "What has happened?" he asked as he noted her red, puffy eyes and tears streaming down her face.

She wearily slumped into a kitchen chair. "Aunt Emily had an accident – she slipped on the ice and broke several bones. Papa does not know if she will walk again."

"I am so sorry," Jeremy took her hand.

"Charlie has had a relapse. He ran in the freezing rain to get help for Aunt Emily. If it was not for him, she could have lain there in the rain for hours. Charlie is burning up with fever and incoherent. What if he dies?" she sobbed. "We cannot help care for Aunt Emily because we are with Charlie."

"Of course, your place is caring for your brother," Mrs. Chase reassured.

"Uncle Danny sent me here to ask if you would consider boarding with them for the winter to help care for my aunt and the boys. He would hate to send them all home. You and Jeremy would have free room and board and he would pay you three dollars a week."

"You tell your uncle that we will be there first thing tomorrow morning. Jeremy, please load the wagon with the food stored in the root cellar. No use having all that food go to waste with a house full of hungry boys."

"What about the livestock?" Jeremy asked.

"We will sell them. I know you do not wish to spend the rest of your life being a farmer."

"Uncle Eli would buy them," Mahayla offered.

"We will use those proceeds to help pay our doctor bills," Jeremy stated.

"Please tell your aunt and uncle that Jeremy and I will be there tomorrow in time to prepare dinner."

X

Long Road to Recovery

The congregation was filled with whispers at the sight of the two empty rows of pews at the front of the church. Reverend Stone wearily walked up the steps to the pulpit.

"Friends, the Miller family needs our prayers. Two days ago, when most of the family was visiting their aunt, Mrs. Daniel Miller fell down the icy back steps of her home breaking her leg, hip, and several ribs. She would have remained there outside in the freezing rain for hours, if her nephew, Charlie had not run to get help. That dear child braved the elements without his coat. Now he is seriously ill in bed with a relapse.

Let us begin our service with prayer."

It was two o'clock that afternoon when Daniel and Jacob came to visit Charlie.

The child slowly opened his eyes. "Grandpa, you came to visit us! Charlie Doll was feeling lonely."

"Are you feeling better today?" the elderly man sounded hopeful as he sat on the side of the bed and took Charlie's hand.

"Just tired." He covered his mouth and he coughed violently.

"Charlie, I came to thank you for being so brave and saving Aunt Emily's life. I am very sorry that you are sick."

"I am not stupid. I am a blessing. Grandpa told me that I am a blessing." He coughed again.

"Your grandfather is a wise man. You are a blessing," Daniel agreed.

"Who is taking care of Aunt Emily?"

"Mrs. Chase and Jeremy have moved in to help us. Between your father and Mrs. Chase and Aunt Rachel, she is receiving excellent care."

"Are you coming over every day to read to me?" Charlie pleaded.

"I am sorry, but I am needed at home."

Charlie sat up in bed. "Uncle Danny, will you read to me now?" He fell fast asleep after the second page.

"Jeremy, you have another wagon load?" Mr. Bennett asked incredulously. He had spent hours yesterday helping Jeremy unload potatoes, apples, squash, carrots, turnips, and baskets of clothing.

"The fresh air and exercise will do you good," Mrs. Chase had assured him.

He doubted that. When he woke up this morning every bone in his body ached.

"Firewood. I intend to pay some of our medical bills with this," he nodded toward the wagon. "I will deliver it to Dr. Miller tomorrow."

Mr. Bennett gave a sigh of relief. "Should you not be in school tomorrow?"

"I am so behind in my studies," he shrugged.

"We will spend evenings studying together and you will be ready to return next semester. We have some time before the other boys return tonight. You can show me how far along you are in your studies and then I can write out a schedule for you."

"We do not accept charity. I will pay you for your tutoring."

"Of course, you will, for my time is valuable. However, I was thinking in terms of pastries. My own dear mother is a terrible cook," he confessed. "In fact, the cook is a terrible cook! My childhood was deprived of cakes and pies and other sweets. Trust me, I shall appreciate the pastries far more than a few coins."

"Well, we have a deal. You get some applesauce, and I will get my books."

After an hour studying in the dining room Mr. Bennett commented, "You have a fine mind, Jeremy."

"Latin comes easily to me. I find Greek to be more challenging."

"Have you thought about attending college?"

"I thought I wanted to become a doctor. Now I am not sure," he confessed.

"Jeremy, you are back!" one of the boys greeted excitedly.

A second boy entered, "We missed you. Are you returning to school?"

"Next semester. I am going to help my mother and Mr. Miller for a while."

"Your mother?"

"Yes, she and I are living here to help out."

"Your mother is going to cook? This day keeps getting better."

Mr. Bennett returned the empty bowls to the kitchen with a sense of satisfaction. Jeremy was both intelligent and popular.

The next morning Jeremy entered the patients' waiting room to discuss his bill with Mrs. Miller.

"Jeremy, Dr. Miller and I are so thankful that you and your mother have decided to move in with Danny and Emily," Lydia warmly greeted. "Should you be in school?"

"Yes, mam. Next semester. I have come to make payment arrangements for my father's bill. I have two cords of firewood in the wagon which I can stack in your woodshed."

"Well, that should just about cover it," she smiled.

"I heard Charlie is sick. Could I go upstairs to visit him?"

"I am sure he would appreciate it."

"Jeremy! You came. I am sick."

"I know. I heard you were brave and got help for your aunt."

"I was very brave. Hayley said you are living with Uncle Danny now and will go back to school. She was very happy."

"I am happy, too." Jeremy smiled.

Jeremy found the house to be lonely and quiet Thanksgiving morning, for the rest of the boys had returned to their homes the day before.

Mrs. Chase brought in a tray of oatmeal and tea in for Emily. "How are you feeling this morning, Mrs. Miller?"

"Tired."

"It is the morphine that makes her sleepy," Daniel explained. "Do try to eat a little," he cajoled.

"I was not planning to have a large Thanksgiving celebration this year due to circumstances," Mrs. Chase explained.

"Every meal you cook is a blessing, Mrs. Chase. I am looking forward to a quiet day."

It was quite another scene at the home of Eli Miller. Julia and her daughter Becky had been cooking and baking since daybreak. Eli, Jonathon, and the older boys went hunting. The girls, entrusted to feeding the chickens and milking the cows, were constantly in and out of the house talking and laughing. As the grandfather clock struck nine, Eli proudly returned with a six- point buck.

"Julia, we will be feasting on venison this month," he laughed. He looked around the kitchen. "Where is my father?"

"I have not seen him all morning. I thought he went hunting with you," she explained. "Is he still in bed?"

✳

"Jonathan, is anything wrong?" Lydia asked.

"Yes, mam. We need Dr. Miller to come right away. His father is having a spell."

A disheveled Isaac ran all the way to the old farmhouse with his black bag in one hand and his hat in the other. "Pa how are you feeling?" he panted as he entered his elderly father's bedroom. Jacob sat in his old chair silently staring out the window. "I will take it from here, Eli. Thank you." Isaac closed the bedroom door. "Are you thinking about Mama? This is a trying time for all of us I fear."

"She read the letter. She knew and she loved me anyway," A tear trickled down his cheek. "I should have told her the truth. But I promised my father I would never tell."

"How did you find the letter?" Isaac had always wanted to ask that since his father showed him the letter after his return from the war.

"You know I was not a good student as a boy."

"No, but you were a good farmer."

"My father insisted that I do my schoolwork at his desk in his office to avoid distractions. One day I made a big smudge in my copy book, so I looked through his drawers for a clean sheet of paper when I saw the letter. I knew it was wrong to open it, but I did it anyway. I could not believe my eyes.

I, Benjamin James Miller, of the town of Fryeburg, in the Province of Maine, in the Commonwealth of Massachusetts, hereby grant complete freedom, Hannah Chase, formerly known as Royal Randolph, who was purchased by me from Mr. and Mrs. Henry Chase of Philadelphia on August, 1792 intending to convey any and all rights of free citizenship of these United States of America.

Benjamin James Miller, Esq.

April 2, 1793

"I promised my father that I would never expose his secret."

"You showed me the letter. You told me," Isaac contradicted.

"What choice did I have? When you returned from the war, I feared you had lost more than your leg. You lost your reason for continuing. I had to show you what you were fighting for. I know some soldiers become so melancholy that they take their lives. I could not let that happen to you."

Isaac felt his heart racing at the image of his nephew's body hanging from the barn's rafters burned in his memory. If only he had shared the secret with David.

"Grandpa was a meticulous man. Why did he leave the letter to be found? Perhaps he hoped someone else would discover the secret without him revealing it? Perhaps it is time to tell the family?"

"Never! Marrying a slave was illegal. He could have gone to jail. What would people think of him breaking the law and marrying a slave from Philadelphia?"

"They are both dead. Slavery has been abolished. What do we care what people think of him?"

"What will people think of us?"

"It did not change Mama's mind about you. That is all that really matters."

"What if Harriet betrays my secret? The whole town of Fryeburg will know."

"Aunt Harriet will not be telling any secrets. She died early this morning."

"Are you sure? Is she really dead?"

Isaac tried not to laugh. "That is exactly what cousin George said to me. He made me wait fifteen minutes before he was convinced that she was dead. Would you like to spend a quiet day at my house? Put on your hat and overcoat and we will take a brisk walk back to my house."

"Walking was a good idea. I believe I am feeling better."

"I am a doctor you know."

"No, you are your mother's son. You are like her in so many ways."

"Mahayla is also like her. She told me she wants to become a doctor. I hope to convince her that owning and operating an apothecary would be more suitable. She can continue her grandmother's legacy."

"And marry the Chase boy?" Jacob added knowingly.

Isaac changed the subject as he turned to Daniel's backyard. "I should stop in and check up on Emily."

"I just stopped by to check on Emily," Isaac explained to Mrs. Chase.

"She is awake in her room."

Isaac found Emily sitting up in the middle of several pillows.

"You are looking much better today," Isaac announced cheerfully. "Tomorrow we will get the old chair on wheels that Mama used. I think getting out of this room and into the parlor and eating in the dining room will do you a world of good. I see no reason why you cannot do some sewing or knitting."

She brightened. "Yes, I agree. Danny, perhaps Eli and Jonathon can bring the chair over from the farm."

"I will do that first thing tomorrow morning," her husband promised.

"Before I forget. Aunt Harriet died last night. Pa had one of his spells and he is coming to my house for dinner. Charlie is up and dressed. I think in time, my two patients will make a complete recovery."

———❉———

Father and son entered the kitchen. "Something smells good," Isaac complimented as he took off his overcoat. "I am famished. I did not have breakfast. I invited Pa to spend a quiet family dinner with us."

"Grandpa, I made apple fritters, just the way Nana taught me," Mahayla carried the platter into the dining room.

"They are good. They are very good." Charlie agreed with powdered sugar on his lips.

The ladies brought a tureen of squash soup, a basket of buttermilk biscuits, glazed carrots, and left-over ham slices from last night dinner. According to family tradition, they took turns saying what they were thankful for.

"Pa, you go first."

"I am thankful that my children and grandchildren live nearby."

"I am thankful that Aunt Emily and Charlie are getting better every day."

"I am thankful Jeremy will be returning to school."

"I am thankful for my children."

"I am thankful that Mr. Lewis and Reverend Stone come to visit me.

"We indeed have much to be thankful."

Monday evening the boys and Mahayla were seated in Emily's dining room studying for a Latin test. Daniel was reading in the front parlor while Emily and Mrs. Chase knitted scarves for the inmates at the poor farm.

Mr. Bennett interrupted the study session, "Mahayla, do you think Charlie would like some company this evening?"

"I am sure he would he enjoy it. Mr. Lewis left on a trip and Charlie is quite perturbed that he cannot visit."

Mr. Bennett found Charlie and Charlie Doll sitting by the parlor stove. "How are you feeling?"

"Mama says I must be feeling much better because I am always getting into mischief," he confessed.

"Would you like me to read to you?"

"*Swiss Family Robinson*?" Summer looked at the book in his hand. "I will make some tea and perhaps I will listen as well."

Mr. Bennett smiled. He spent every evening during the next three weeks reading to Charlie and Summer.

———❉———

By February Charlie was well enough to resume his school routine of spending mornings with Uncle Danny and afternoons at the General Store. Isaac continued to check in on Emily daily and was relieved to see that she was making slow but steady progress. By spring Charlie felt well enough to weed the herb gardens with Mahayla and visit with his grandfather.

The family was now planning for Summer's upcoming graduation.

XI

Graduation

Once the Miller clan decided they would celebrate with dinner at Emily's dining room, Julia, Becky, and Mrs. Chase were planning and cooking for days. After much correspondence, Mr. Bennett convinced his mother and Lily to visit Fryeburg, attend the graduation, and meet the Millers for dinner. After a brief stay, the three of them would return to Concord.

Jeremy and Charlie were assigned to pick up the ladies at the train station as Mr. Bennett attended to his responsibilities. "Here comes the train!" Charlie called out excitedly. "How will we know it is them? There will be a crowd of people getting off the train."

"Look for two ladies in very fancy dresses and lots of trunks and hat boxes," Jeremy predicted.

"Are they city ladies like I have seen at the Oxford House?"

"Yes. And there they are," he pointed to the two women dressed in large hats, gloves, and voluminous skirts. "You stay in the wagon, and I will fetch them."

"Good afternoon, mam. May I assume you are Mrs. Bennett? Mr. Bennett has arranged for us to escort you to the Oxford

House. He will meet you there this evening for dinner. My name is Jeremy Chase, one of his students and I live at the Miller's boarding house."

"Why isn't Emerson here himself to pick us up?" the younger woman demanded.

"He is not available this afternoon."

"Very well. Where is your carriage?"

"My wagon is over there," he pointed to Charlie who was standing, waving Charlie Doll, and grinning from ear to ear. "I believe the wagon will be better suited to carry your trunks. It is a short ride," he assured them after noting their displeasure.

"My son sent the village simpleton to pick us up," Mrs. Bennett whispered to Lily.

Jeremy pretended not to hear that comment. "I will fetch, I mean locate a porter to assist me with your trunks, mam."

Finally, the two trunks and four hat boxes were loaded in the back. "This is Charlie Miller, Mr. and Mrs. Miller's nephew."

"Mr. Bennett is my teacher too. He read *The Swiss Family Robinson* at night when I was sick. Charlie Doll and I like him very, very much. My mother told me to sit in the back of the wagon and let Mrs. Bennett sit upfront because she is old."

"Miss Lily please allow me to help you to the back. Your trunk will serve as your seat," Jeremy offered.

"Do you expect me to sit in the back like a piece of luggage?" she gasped.

"Do not be afraid! Charlie Doll and I will sit next to you."

Mrs. Bennett and Miss Lily inspected the Oxford House with a discerning eye. They found nothing to criticize as the porters brought their trunks to their rooms. At six o'clock the ladies descended the staircase dressed in their evening attire.

Graduation

"How are my two favorite ladies?" Mr. Bennett greeted. "I trust your journey went well."

"Really Emerson. You send a farm boy and an idiot in a filthy wagon to pick us up? Do you have any idea how humiliating it was arriving in such a conveyance?" his mother scolded.

"That boy should be sent away to an institution!" Lily exclaimed.

Mr. Bennett laughed. "Jeremy told me what happened."

"It is not funny, Emerson."

"You will both feel better after dinner and a good night's sleep."

They quietly studied the menu. "Emerson, I fail to understand why you refused to come home for Christmas. You would rather spend your time with these farmers, than with me?" Lily accused.

"I explained all this is my letters. First traveling was not practical for the academy was closed for just a few days, and I had much to prepare for the next semester. I wrote about Mrs. Miller's serious accident and Charlie's illness. After the students returned home, I felt I could be of service to Mr. Miller by helping with the firewood, shoveling snow, and doing errands."

"That is what servants are for, dear," Mrs. Bennett reminded her son.

"I attended the Christmas Eve reception without an escort. My father insisted I attend after all the money he spent on my gown," Lily stated bitterly.

"Perhaps, you can wear it at our wedding," he innocently smiled.

She rolled her eyes. "Really, Emerson."

"Have you reconsidered working at Bennett Publishing? his mother questioned.

"No, I have not," he replied almost apologetically.

"Are you telling me you plan to spend another year here?" Lily asked in exasperation.

"That is exactly what I plan to do. When you visit the Academy, meet my fellow instructors, my students, and the Miller family, you will understand why I enjoy teaching here. Plus, your father insists I have a sizable bank account before I ask for your hand in marriage."

"That is ridiculous!" Mrs. Bennett stated with indignation. "You are a Bennett! You will inherit the house. Your uncle has offered you a position as a copy editor at the publishing firm. I do not understand why you are so stubborn and insist on teaching in this little town!"

"Just in time," Mr. Bennett greeted the waiter who came to take their order.

The second-floor auditorium was crowded with visitors. Charlie stood up and waved his doll, "Mrs. Bennett, Miss Lily, we saved you a seat!"

With sighs of exasperation and the swishing of their many petticoats the ladies approached Isaac who rose from his seat. "Mrs. Bennett, Miss Lily, I am Dr. Isaac Miller, and this is my wife, Lydia." Mrs. Bennett was surprised by the quality of the doctor's suit. Mrs. Miller's afternoon dress rivaled her own.

"I do apologize for my son's outburst yesterday," Lydia blushed. He is still recovering from rheumatic fever and is not quite himself.

Graduation

Mr. Bennett has been such a help to our family. Charlie simply adores him. When he heard that Jeremy was going to pick you up, I allowed him to go. Against my better judgment. This is our daughter, Mahayla."

"It is nice to make your acquaintance," she replied politely but absent mindedly. Clearly, she was not impressed with the ladies' outfits for she barely glanced at them.

"You can sit with me," Charlie offered. "I did not want you to be lonely. Summer is graduating today. We are having a very big party at Aunt Emily's house. You are invited too." The ladies took their seats as the program began.

Lily stifled a yawn after the third speech. Finally. the headmaster began calling the names of the graduates to receive their diplomas.

"Summer Miller." Headmaster Fiske called.

"That is my sister!" Charlie shouted and the audience chuckled.

Lily gasped as a beautiful young woman with an hourglass figure, dressed in a striking cream color silk dress crossed the stage. Her auburn hair was piled high on her head with ringlets cascading by her face.

After the benediction, the crowd descended the stairs. "There you are, Emerson," Lily called out.

"I see you have met some of the Millers. There are several more to meet," he explained.

"I am so looking forward to it," she smiled sweetly as she slipped her arm through his.

"May I offer you two ladies a ride in my carriage?" Isaac invited.

"That would be lovely," Mrs. Bennett accepted.

"Charlie and I will walk back to Uncle Danny's" Mahayla offered. "The carriage can only accommodate five people."

"Here is our older daughter, Summer," Isaac introduced as he helped her into the carriage.

"Emerson, are you coming?" his mother asked.

"I will walk. The carriage can only hold five people," he reminded.

"Walk with me! Walk with me! Mrs. Chase baked the best cake in the world and Cousin Becky and Jonathan will make ice cream." Charlie grabbed Mr. Bennett's hand and led him off.

Daniel greeted the carriage, "Welcome."

Mrs. Bennet studied the three-story white house with a discerning eye.

Isaac and Daniel led their guests to the front parlor. "Mrs. Chase will bring in some beverages shortly."

"I shall have a glass of white wine, please," Lily ordered.

"I am sorry, but we are a Temperance family. Both my grandparents were abolitionists and founders of our local Temperance Movement," Daniel explained.

"How quaint," Lily commented as she took a seat by the window.

"What an impressive collection of books," Mrs. Bennett complimented as she studied the tomes. "Are these all yours?"

"I am not the owner; I am merely a steward. Most of these belonged to my grandfather, Senator Benjamin Miller. I have had the pleasure of reading many of them," Daniel concluded.

"I see you have some works by Ralph Waldo Emerson. Waldo and my late husband were dear friends."

"May I assume Emerson is named after this gentleman?"

"Emerson is a more dignified name than Ralph, don't you think? Have you had the opportunity to read his essays?"

"I assure you I am no Transcendentalist. I was rather vexed by his philosophies when reading his *Divinity School Address of*

1838. He discounted the Biblical miracles and denied the deity of Christ, claiming Jesus may have been a great man, he certainly was not God. After that I elected not to read his other essays."

"That is rather closed minded, don't you think?" she challenged.

Lydia interrupted, "I think I will bring us some lemonade."

"Let me warn you, Rachel arrived an hour ago."

"Say no more," she laughed. "I will venture into the kitchen and return with our refreshments."

"Is Rachel one of your servants?" Lily inquired.

"Rachel is our sister. She and her husband own the large general store across from the hotel."

"A shop keeper. How quaint," Lily commented.

"Dr. Miller, do you enjoy reading as well?" Mrs. Bennett turned to Isaac. "I am sure a man of science such as yourself, is not bound by traditions and superstitions."

"My reading is strictly limited to medical journals. I am studying Louis Pasteur's germ theory and the writings of Dr. Edward Jenner, the inventor of the smallpox vaccine. I believe vaccines are the future of medicine. I hope we have a tetanus vaccine within my lifetime. I just lost a patient…"

Daniel loudly cleared his throat. "That may be an indelicate discussion in the presence of ladies."

Lydia and Mrs. Chase returned with two trays of pitchers of lemonade and delicate teacups. "Lunch will commence shortly," Lydia announced as Mrs. Chase began filling cups and serving the guests.

"What are your lovely daughter's plans after graduation?" Mrs. Bennett asked Lydia.

"I tell you I would not be able to run my husband's office without her."

"She was a great help when Charlie was so ill," Isaac added.

"She is meticulously organized. I do not know how she finds time to read so many books and now she is writing her first novel. She plans to continue to assist me in the office and to write."

"And your other daughter?" Lily quickly changed the focus of the conversation.

Isaac laughed. "Mahayla is clearly my daughter. She grew up helping her grandmother in her herb garden, as I did. She plans to open her own apothecary."

"Here they are," Daniel stood as Mahayla, Charlie, and Emerson entered the foyer.

"Mama, I am hungry. I am very, very hungry. Is it time to eat?" Charlie asked.

"It certainly is." Lydia led the guests from the front parlor to the dining room.

"Mother, Lily, this is Mrs. Miller," Emerson introduced the woman in the wheeled chair.

"Welcome to our home," Emily greeted. Please take a seat." She pointed to the name cards on a table by the window.

Summer came over and kissed her aunt on the cheek. "Aunt Emily, what a beautiful reception. First you made this lovely dress and now this! I simply do not know how to thank you."

Mrs. Bennett surveyed the tables covered in white linens, set with fine China and crystal goblets. Each table had a vase of forsythia.

"You have your Aunt Rachel to thank for the table settings. They are on loan from the store."

"The next table is reserved for you, your family and Jeremy. Aunt Rachel and Uncle Peter will be joining Grandpa, Uncle Eli, Aunt Julia, Becky, and Jonathan. The cousins are eating outdoors on a table. Charlie, after dinner you may join them outside and make ice cream."

"Ice cream is good, very good," Charlie muttered as found his seat.

Daniel and Emerson sat at each end of the table, with Mrs. Bennett and Lily seated across. Daniel stood to say grace. "Heavenly Father, we thank you for all your good gifts, especially the gift of your only Son who died for our sins. As we celebrate the graduation of Summer, we ask that your Holy Spirit guide her paths and help her to become the godly woman you wish her to be.

Thank you for this abundance of food, for this family and for blessing us with such good cooks. In Jesus precious name we pray."

"Amen. Can we eat now?" Charlie asked.

"Did I understand correctly that you sewed Summer's dress?" Lily asked sweetly.

"It was Rachel's idea. She purchased bolts of that Parisian silk and suggested I make a dress for Summer."

"I do not know how your sister-in-law does it!" Mrs. Chase remarked.

"She has connections in New York City. She knew if the ladies of Fryeburg saw Summer in that dress, they would come to the store to buy the fabric. What an extravagance at nine yards per dress! I do hope these silly fashions change to something more reasonable," Emily exclaimed not realizing the insult to her guests.

Lily felt her cheeks blushing. "I understand that since Queen Victoria married in a white gown. Wearing white at your wedding is becoming quite fashionable. Mrs. Miller, may I employ

The Fryeburg Chronicles Book VI

you to make my wedding gown from that fabric?" she smiled demurely at Emerson. "My father will pay you handsomely."

"No thank you. Sewing is my ministry and not my profession," Emily rejected.

"My dear wife has devoted her life to sewing clothes for the needy and teaching other women how to sew. She occasionally sews for a family member should the need arise."

"Lily there are many fine dressmakers in Concord," Mrs. Bennett added.

"This food is simply superb. I dare say this meal is finer than last night's dinner at the hotel," Emerson changed the subject.

"Yes. My compliments to the chef," Mrs. Bennett added.

"My sister-in-law, Julia is probably the best cook in Fryeburg. She has won many blue ribbons at the Fryeburg Fair for her pies, pickles, and jams."

"How quaint."

"It is good to see my father laughing again," Daniel changed the subject. "We lost our mother almost a year ago. The two of them were inseparable. I fear the family is still grieving."

"That is one reason why we decided to hold this reception. We needed a family celebration," Emily continued.

At the conclusion of the luncheon, Charlie came running to the table. "Mrs. Chase, we are ready to go outside and make ice cream. Can I help Jeremy get the cream from the root cellar?"

"No, you may not, young man. I will go with some of the other boys. You wait outside for us. Please excuse me," Mrs. Chase left the table.

"I do admire you for your progressive ideas. Not many ladies allow the help to eat with them," Lily observed.

Daniel intervened before Emily could open her mouth. "Mrs. Chase is not a servant. She is an answer to prayer. The day of Emily's accident, I realized I could not possibly house and feed a houseful of young men. Mrs. Chase graciously left her farm to come to live with us, care for Emily and do the cooking and cleaning. I do not know what we would have done without her all these months."

After finishing their cake and ice cream Mrs. Bennett complimented "Mrs. Miller, I commend you for a fine dinner party,".

"I am pleased that you were able to join our little family celebration. Would you like Mr. Miller to take you back to the hotel in his carriage?"

As the ladies stood up to leave, Summer approached the table.

"Mr. Bennett, may I impose upon your good nature? I have just finished a novel about a young woman who left the farm to work in a textile mill. I would be honored if you could read it over the summer and give me your thoughts upon your return."

"Miss Miller, I assure you that it will be my pleasure," Mr. Bennett replied warmly.

"Thank you, sir. Mrs. Chase, please have another slice of cake and cup of tea. Charlie, Mahayla, and I are going to go home, change our clothes, and return to wash the dishes," Summer informed. "All of you have worked so hard. This is the least I can do."

"I can wash dishes. I am very good at washing dishes," Charlie boasted. "Is there any ice cream left?"

---❈---

Two days later Daniel escorted Mrs. Bennett, Lily, and Emerson to the train station in his carriage as Jeremy and Charlie arrived in the wagon filled with trunks.

The train came to a stop. "Are you coming back, Mr. Bennett?" Charlie sniffled.

"Yes, I will return in August and you, and Jeremy will meet me. Here is my address," he handed Charlie a slip of paper. "I expect you to write me a letter next week."

"Writing is hard, very hard," he complained.

"Summer will help you. And she will read this to you," he handed him a book.

"*The Adventures of Tom Sawyer*. Is this for me?"

"Open up the cover."

"To Benjamin Charles Miller from Emerson James Bennett 1876"

"Does this book belong to me? This is good, very, very good."

Once the trunks and passengers boarded the train, Charlie stood on the wagon waving Charlie Doll. Mr. Bennett stuck his head out the window and waved back.

XII

Vienna, Austria

American Journalist, Thaddeus Pierce, inconspicuously entered the crowded hall and found an empty chair in the back of the room. He was grateful that he had brushed up on his German, as the night's speaker, Josef Szadkowski, began his speech on the coming Socialist Revolution. The earnest young man meticulously covered all talking points:

Abolition of private property
A heavy progressive income tax
Abolition of all right of inheritance
Confiscation of all property of emigrants and rebels
Centralization of credit in the hands of the state
Centralization of means of communication and transportation in the hands of the state
Extension of factories and instruments of production owned by the state
Equal obligation of all to work
Gradual abolition of all the distinctions between town and country by a more equitable distribution of the population over the country
Free education for all children in public schools.[1.]

The audience of mostly young men rose to their feet clapping and cheering. Twenty-eight years ago, Pierce would have joined them; now he was older and wiser. He realized that terror would be necessary to implement such a truly radical, totalitarian ideology. This philosophy demanded an unequivocal rejection of the most basic rights, including property.[2] He waited for the hall to clear out before approaching the speaker.

"That was quite the speech, Herr Szadkowski," the middle-aged man greeted.

"That is quite a compliment coming from an American capitalist."

"How did you know?"

"Your German is impeccable, but your accent is terrible."

"Have you ever met Karl Marx?"

"Why no. But I have read everything he has written."

"I have interviewed him a dozen times over the past twenty-five years. I am writing a biography."

The young man now gave Pierce his undivided attention. "What did you say your name was?"

"Excuse me. Thaddeus Pierce," he handed Josef his business card."

"I cannot read English," he returned the card.

"I am a journalist for an American newspaper called the New York Post. Now that my interviews with Marx are completed, I am investigating his followers."

"What is he like?"

"Let me buy you a beer and I will tell you anything you like." The two walked back to the bar at Pierce's hotel. After ordering a beer and a Scotch the men took a seat at a corner table.

"What is he like?" Josef repeated.

"He smells!"

Vienna, Austria

The young man laughed. "Your German is not so good after all. You just said he smells."

"He does. He smells. He stinks. He doesn't bathe. He is covered with boils. He never worked for a day in his life. He drinks too much. He refuses to care for his wife and children."[3.]

"Is he married? I thought he wanted to abolish the family?"

"He doesn't want the responsibility of caring for them. He envisions the state caring for children. He came from a successful business family. He is Jewish on both sides of the family with a few ancestors who were rabbis. His father converted to Protestantism, Lutheran, I believe. It was better for business connections. Anyway, family notwithstanding, he is quite the bigot! You should hear some of the antisemitic language he uses. Did you ever read his essay he wrote back in 44 'On the Jewish Question'"?[4.]

"Why no," Josef stammered.

"By the way, I would change my last name if I was you, Josef. Something less Polish, less Jewish, if you want to move up in the ranks."

Josef looked puzzled. "As I was saying. I heard Jenny, Mrs. Marx, tell him, 'Karl, if only you had spent more time making capital instead of writing about it.'[5.] His wife and children lived in poverty. He left Jenny to face the wrath of the landlord, the grocer, the butcher, and the pub as they all demanded she pay the debts. Their one-year-old son died from neglect during the bitter cold winter of 1850.[6.]

He demanded that his father assist his family financially. Then after not attending his father's funeral, he demanded that his widowed mother help support them as well. For a man who wants to abolish inheritance, he had no problem accepting $6,000 in gold and francs after his mother died.[7]

Have you heard of Fredrich Engels?"

"Of course."

"He is the one who basically supports the Marx family.[8.] Which is interesting, because, he never had his own family, just a series of mistresses – sometime several at the same time. I guess that is why he also wanted to abolish the family."

"Where did Mr. Engels get the money?"

"His family owned a textile mill in Manchester, England. You see socialism needs to be financed by capitalists. Where else will the money come from?"

Josef opened his mouth as if to argue, but he could think of nothing to say.

"Are you a religious Jew?"

"Certainly not! Religion is the opiate of the masses," he quoted Marx.

"Good. Both Marx and Engels claim to be atheists, but communism is their new religion.[9.] Their focus is materialism not the soul. 'Man does not live by bread alone'…"

"Your Jesus said that, not mine," Josef interrupted.

"Impressive for the grandson of a famous rabbi."

"How do you know my grandfather?"

"I met him once. He threw me out of his house."

Josef burst out laughing.

"As I was saying… Instead of believing in heaven, they believe in a man-made utopia.[9] As Augustine, the Bishop of Hippo said, "We all have a God-shaped vacuum that God alone can fill. We cannot be satisfied by materialism. We crave divine manna of heaven."[10.]

"You are quite the religious man, aren't you Herr Pierce."

"My grandmother was a very godly woman, but I rejected everything she taught me. Now I am beginning to think perhaps

Vienna, Austria

she was right," he sighed. "Marx and Engels believe that the answers to man's miseries are not found in God, but in economic materialism. If that is true, why are some rich people miserable and some simple people happy? Yes, people need food, shelter, and jobs to be productive. But more importantly, people need family, faith, and love."

"Why are you telling me all this?" he demanded.

"I don't want you to waste your life on…"

"It's my life to waste!" he stood up.

"Your mother was a socialist."

He immediately sat down. "What did you say?"

"I knew your mother when we were both living in Paris, back in 1848."

"That's impossible. She never left Poland."

"Did your grandfather tell you that? I knew your mother very well. We didn't know she was with child when I left for Ireland to report on the potato famine, then left for America and traveled for months. It took almost two years for her letters to be delivered to me. By then, she had returned to Poland in disgrace, gave birth to twins, and died a few weeks later."

"But my father was a rabbi who died before we were born!"

"Did your grandfather tell you that?"

"Why are you telling me this? After all these years, what right do you have to show up now?"

"You and your brother are in danger. I have been traveling all through Europe and I see the wave of antisemitism building – particularly in eastern Europe. There are massacres of Jews. The Russians call them pogroms. You and your brother are the only close family I have left. I want you to come to America with me and start a new life where you will be safe. I wanted to take both of you back to America when you were two years old.

Your grandfather refused. I gave him all the money I had to care for you and then he threw me out. I lost track of you after he moved several times. I speak very poor Polish and no Yiddish, but I never gave up searching."

"Natan has a wife and three children in Warsaw."

"I would take all of them with me. Warsaw is a very large city. How will I find them?"

"Buy me a round trip train ticket and I will take you there."

XIII

Warsaw, Poland

Thaddeus was most grateful Josef had accompanied him on this journey, for he surely would have gotten lost in the maze of streets in this busy, crowded city.

"They will not be home at this time of day. The girls will be in school and Natan and Miriam will be at the shop," Josef explained in German as people spoke unfamiliar Yiddish. Thaddeus was out of breath as they stopped in front of a shop with two large windows displaying men's suits and women's elegant dresses. He could not read the sign over the shop's door. A bell quietly rang as they stepped into the immaculate showroom.

The woman behind the counter greeted Josef with angry words and the two argued before he pointed to Thaddeus. The woman immediately left for a back room and disappeared behind the closed door. Moments later a young man appeared dressed in a black suit and a yarmulke. Clearly the brothers were not identical twins, for Natan had the Millers' curly brown hair, grey eyes.

"Shalom. Please forgive me for this intrusion while you are busy at work, but it is urgent that I speak with you," Thaddeus addressed him in Hebrew.

"You speak Hebrew?" Josef asked incredulously.

"Doesn't everyone?" Thaddeus retorted. Natan laughed and invited them to his workroom.

"I can't wait to see the expression on his face when you tell him," Josef whispered in German.

"My name is Thaddeus Pierce, and I am a journalist from America," he introduced himself. "I see you are a tailor," Thaddeus observed the shelves holding bolts of luxurious fabrics. "Did you make all the clothing displayed in the windows? You are a talented man. America needs talented men like you."

"Why would I leave my home, my synagogue, and my successful business to start over in a land of gentiles? You came all the way from America to offer me a job? Why?" he asked suspiciously.

Thaddeus took a deep breath. "I met your grandfather, Rabbi Szadkowski, when you and your brother were about two years old. He told me that both your parents had died, and he and his wife were raising you."

"Yes, they did. God rest their souls. They provided us with a loving, Godly upbringing, which only one of us appreciates," he glared at Josef who stood there smirking.

"Grandparents are a blessing! I lived with my parents and my grandparents Hannah and Benjamin. They were very wise, and I wish I had listened to them when I was a younger man. Your grandfather was a respected rabbi; my grandfather was a respected attorney, judge, and United States senator." Both young men looked impressed.

"They were my mother's parents, and their last name was Miller. Your grandfather was the father of your mother. Why do you not have your father's name? Have you ever met your father's family?"

Warsaw, Poland

"Well, no," Natan stammered. "I never really thought about it. We grew up with many aunts, uncles, cousins plus members of the synagogue who were like family. I guess I never thought about it."

"It sounds like your grandparents blessed you with a happy childhood. Now that you are a father, you can understand how adults may choose to shield children from the truth to protect them. Your grandfather was ashamed of your heritage."

"Why should he be…"

"What the man is trying to tell you," Josef interrupted, "he is our father!"

"That is impossible! Our grandfather would never let his daughter marry a gentile!"

"Who said anything about marriage?" Josef snickered.

Natan turned pale before speaking excitedly in Yiddish.

"I don't know what you are saying," Thaddeus interrupted in Hebrew, "but it sounds very similar to what your grandfather said before he threw me out of his house. Your mother and I met in Paris back in 48. We were both young, rebellious, far from home and thought we had all the answers. She didn't speak English, and I don't speak Yiddish, but we both spoke French. We did not know that she was with child, when I left for Ireland, and then for various cities in America. She wrote me several letters, but I did not receive them for almost two years. Her last letter said she had no choice but to return to Poland.

By the time I located you, your grandfather told me she had died a few weeks after giving birth to twins. They fabricated a story about her husband, a rabbi, dying. I wanted to take both of you home with me to America. I would have made a terrible father, but you would have had grandparents and great-grandparents and many other relatives who loved you! I left him all the money I had for your care and left. When I tried to visit several years later, your family had moved."

"So, what do you want from me? Money?" Natan snapped.

"No. As I explained to your brother, I have travelled a great deal throughout Europe. I can see that antisemitism is growing. I want to pay for you and your family to come back to America where you will be safe."

"That is ridiculous. Our family has lived in Poland for generations, for centuries. We are in no danger here."

"Perhaps not from other Polish citizens. What about the Russians? Your borders are not easily defended," Thaddeus argued.

"I do not need your money! If danger comes, I will sell my home, my business, take my money out of the bank. Unlike you, I know how to care for my family!"

"Under ordinary circumstances, you can. What happens when every Jewish family in Poland is trying to sell their home or business? What happens if Poland is invaded, and the banks are closed?" Thaddeus challenged.

"I'm not worried. I'm changing my name to Joe Pierce," Josef laughed.

Thaddeus ignored him. "This is why I want to give you this money to hide and keep in case you and your family need to flee." He opened his satchel and handed him a muslin bag of gold coins, train and ship itineraries written in Hebrew."

"Don't I get any money?" Josef complained.

"Get a job!" Thaddeus retorted.

A side door slowly opened, and a four-year-old boy entered. "Are you really my grandfather?" he asked shyly.

Thaddeus' heart melted as he knelt beside his grandson. "What is your name?" he asked tenderly.

"Joshua."

"That is the name of my father."

"Were you eavesdropping? Miriam!" Natan called.

"I am ashamed to admit that we were both eavesdropping," his wife entered the room.

"I want to go to America. Give me the money and I will take Mama and my sisters with me."

"Natan, please. What if this man is right? Please take the money. Do it for me. Do it for the children," Miriam pleaded.

Thaddeus handed the bag to his grandson. "You promise not to tell anyone? Not even your sisters?"

The child nodded.

"When I get to New York City, I will purchase two Yiddish/English dictionaries and mail you one. We will write letters. I will teach you English."

"I will teach you Yiddish!" Joshua added. "Are you really my grandfather?" he repeated.

Thaddeus looked at Natan. "Yes, he is your grandfather. If your grandfather wants to give his only grandson a gift, who am I to disagree?"

Thaddeus was unsure if he gained a family or lost a fortune.

XIV

Cousin Thaddeus

Ten-year-old Charlie covered his ears as the locomotive neared the Fryeburg train station. He was excited to accompany Jeremy to pick up Mr. Bennett returning from his summer in Concord, Massachusetts. He held Charlie Doll in one hand and several letters in the other as he watched the train pull to a stop and passengers disembark.

"I see him!" Charlie stood up in the wagon and waved Charlie Doll in the air. "Mr. Bennett! Mr. Bennett!"

Mr. Bennett waved back and headed to the wagon.

"I came to pick you up! I read and kept all your letters!" Charlie waved them.

"I read and kept your letters as well. I thank you two gentlemen for coming. I would have been content to walk but I have two trunks of books and items."

"I can help you with those," Jeremy offered. "Charlie, you stay with the horses."

"Horses are good."

It took a half hour before the trunks were unloaded from the train and reloaded onto the back of the wagon.

"Sir, did you enjoy your summer," Jeremy asked.

"It was good to be home with friends and family. However, I missed my students, Mrs. Chase's cooking, Mr. and Mrs. Miller's company, and above all teaching. It is good to be back. How was your summer?"

"Summer was busy, very busy," Charlie interrupted. "Me and Hayley and Jeremy spent every day in Nana's gardens. But now they are Hayley's gardens. Hayley says I am a good worker, a very good worker. Grandpa says I am good company. He tells me stories about when he was a little boy. That was a long time ago, a very long time ago. Aunt Emily can walk with a cane, but she needs Mrs. Chase's help."

A well-dressed, middle-aged gentleman carrying two leather valises approached them. "Good day. May I hire you to take me to the home of Mr. Daniel Miller?"

"Uncle Danny's house! You know Uncle Danny?"

"I am his cousin, Thaddeus Pierce."

"I am Benjamin Charles Miller. Everybody calls me Charlie."

"You must be Isaac's son."

"Sir, we are all on our way to the house. I am Jeremy Chase. My mother and I live there."

"Emerson Bennett, instructor at the Academy. I board there during the school year, as well."

"Cousin Thaddeus, you can sit in back with me and Charlie Doll," he invited.

As the wagon stopped at the Miller's stables Charlie jumped out and ran into the house shouting, "Cousin Thaddeus has come for a visit!"

Emily laughed, "Who is coming for a visit?"

Thaddeus entered the kitchen, "I am. Uncle Jacob wrote of your accident. I am pleased to see that you are up and about."

Daniel entered the kitchen, "The prodigal has returned! We have not seen you since the war. How long do you plan to stay?"

"I would like to stay several months. I was hoping perhaps I may stay with you?"

"The Lord has given us this home and He continues to bring people to fill it," Daniel smiled. "May I introduce you to Mrs. Chase? She graciously moved in the day after Emily's accident to help. We now have decided that we cannot live without her."

"Would you like tea and biscuits in the front parlor?" she offered.

"We have one empty bedroom left downstairs. Follow me and I will help you get settled."

Thaddeus turned to Charlie, "Do you think you could invite your grandfather and Uncle Eli to join us? Is your father busy?"

"I will get them. I can run fast. I was sick, very sick, but now I am better. I will invite Aunt Rachel too."

Daniel nodded. "We will never hear the end of it, if we do not."

Charlie ignored the chickens roaming the front yard, ran up the front steps and through the front door. He found Jacob sitting in the parlor sadly staring through the window at his Kate's herb gardens.

"Grandpa, you and Uncle Eli are invited for tea at Uncle Danny's house. Cousin Thaddeus is here."

"Thaddeus? I have not seen him since '63."

"Where does he live?"

"He lives everywhere and nowhere in particular. The last I heard from him he was in Europe. He must have returned home for the election. Tell Uncle Danny, we will be there shortly."

When Jacob and Eli arrived, they found Isaac and Rachel also visiting. Thaddeus stood to greet his uncle, "Uncle Jacob, I was so sorry to hear of Aunt Kate's passing. What a loss for the entire family," he warmly shook his hand. Eli, I was sorry to hear about David's death."

"Julia and I will always be grateful that you brought him home to us. It was a great comfort to have him with us for a few months before his death."

"We are all grateful to you for bringing home an Irish orphan almost thirty years ago," Daniel added. "Like it or not, you are an important part of our family."

"I am sorry that I have spent years away from home, not being here for births, weddings, and deaths."

"The important thing is you are here now," Jacob assured.

"I need my family now. You have always taken in people in need. My family needs your help."

"Thaddeus, you have a family?" Rachel exclaimed. "Why is it you have never brought them here? Why have you not spoken of them before?"

He relayed the story to his family. "Their grandfather the rabbi never told them about me."

"A rabbi? Do you mean he's Jewish?" Eli asked.

"Not only was he Jewish, but my sons are also Jewish. I lost track of them because they moved several times over the decades. After searching for them for years, I found them last month!"

"Mercy! How? Where?" Rachel was enthralled.

"I met Josef in Vienna where he was involved with organizing a Socialist Movement."

"The acorn does not fall far from the tree," Jacob interjected.

"He is estranged from his religion, brother and family."

"Did you tell him who you are? How did he respond?"

"He laughed to think that both of his parents were socialists. My other son, Natan, did not take the news very well. He was angry at me for abandoning his mother, angry at his grandfather for not telling them the truth, and embarrassed about his parentage. I met Natan's wife Miriam and his son, Joshua. The two girls were at school. I gave him all the money I had on me and your address and begged him to bring his wife and children with him to live in America, in Fryeburg."

"Why? Do they not have a home in Poland?"

"On the contrary, Natan is quite prosperous. However, the tide of anti-Semitism is rapidly rising in Russia and Eastern Europe. I fear for their lives. My parents are gone; I have no siblings. They are my family. I need to protect and provide for them."

"If we can take in the Irish, we certainly can take in the Polish," Emily stated.

"I can provide the extra food," Eli volunteered.

"Free medical care and plenty of hand-me-down clothing," Isaac added.

"We will pray for the Lord's protection until He leads them to us." Daniel settled the matter.

Isaac returned to his office where two patients were waiting; Rachel returned to her store where Peter and several customers were waiting. Eli invited his cousin for supper that evening.

"Next month I am leaving for Philadelphia to report on the 1876 Centennial Exhibition. I would like to invite the three of you to join me as my guests.

"What is this exhibition?" Eli asked.

"Think of it as a giant Fryeburg Fair–a fair on 285 acres in one of our oldest and busiest cities. There will be exhibits from every state and many foreign countries and new inventions on display."[1.] Turning to Julia he added, "There is a women's pavilion as well."

"It would be great to see the new farming trends and new inventions," Eli stated enthusiastically.

"I have never taken a train before. My parents lived in Philadelphia before they were married. It would be quite an adventure." For the first time since Kate's death Jacob had something to look forward to. "Jonathan and Becky can run the farm. Julia, you deserve a vacation. When do we leave?"

"In a few weeks.

One evening Mr. Bennett called on Summer at home.

"Did you enjoy your time with your family?" she asked politely.

"I did, thank you. However, I was eager to return to Fryeburg by midsummer. I had plenty of time to read your manuscript. That is why I am here this evening."

Summer put down her fountain pen and looked into his eyes. "I would appreciate your honest evaluation."

"You have a command of the English language. Your descriptions of the boarding house, the mill, and the machinery were extraordinary! I felt as if I was there. However, your character development was somewhat lacking. What was the protagonist thinking? What was she feeling? Why would she leave home? I did not feel as if I knew her well."

"Perhaps it is because you are a man who would not understand a woman's need for some independence."

"That may very well be true," he admitted. "It felt like you were telling someone else's story, not your own. Because you did not know the character well, the reader could not know her well."

"Point well taken," Summer conceded. "This is the story of when Aunt Rachel left to work in Biddeford for a few years."

He nodded. "I was unsure of the plot. She came, she worked, she returned home. Was she a reformer? Did she earn enough money to live independently?"

Summer looked crestfallen. "I thank you for your time. That was kind of you."

"You have talent Miss Miller. I do hope you will continue writing. Select a story and make it your own. What do you feel passionately about? Draw your readers into your world and do not leave them on the outside merely observing. Make your readers care about your characters. You are a young woman. Perhaps in a few years, when you have had more life experiences, more challenges, more depth, more maturity. Please continue writing. Good evening, Miss Miller."

"Good evening, sir."

Jacob entered the family parlor, where Daniel and Thaddeus were waiting.

"I realize I know little about my parents. Uncle Jacob, what was my mother like growing up?"

"She was very bright and did well in school. She was like your grandfather in many ways. She was always reading books, worked as an instructress at the Academy and helped your grandfather in the office."

Cousin Thaddeus

"I remember she was a terrible cook. I would have starved if we did not live with Nana," Thaddeus exaggerated.

"Your grandmother was certain Abigail would be an old maid. She did not show interest in any of the young men in Fryeburg."

"Until she met my father."

"Of course not. We were both children when Joshua worked for my father the first time."

"The first time?"

"Yes. After Daniel Webster left…"

"Do you mean Senator Daniel Webster who served as Secretary of State under three Presidents?"

"He was not famous back then. He was just a young attorney who served as the Headmaster of Fryeburg Academy and made some extra money writing up deeds for Mr. Osgood as well as assisting my father. After he left, my father was overburdened with responsibilities and hired this young farmer from southern New Hampshire who just graduated from Dartmouth College."

"I never knew he grew up on a farm."

"He was one of seven sons and a humble and hardworking man. He lived at the Oxford House but had meals with us. After a few years he left and had quite a successful law practice in Salem, Massachusetts. He returned to Fryeburg on the day of my grandfather's funeral in 1819.

"Why would he leave his own practice to return here?" Thaddeus asked incredulously.

"Tragedy. He lost his wife, children, law practice, and his home in a house fire. He lost everything."

"I never knew that! Do you mean he had an entire family that he never talked about?"

"You have a family that you never talked about," Jacob observed. "I assume it was too painful to discuss. When my grandfather, James, heard the devastating news he began writing to him, and invited him to come live on the farm.

Joshua arrived the day of my grandfather's funeral. My grandmother convinced him that the family desperately needed his help on the farm. By now Kate and I were married. She and I and the boys were still living with my parents, while I helped Uncle Micah on the farm. Abigail was serving as my father's assistant. She did just about everything a lawyer could do.

My father was a judge and Joshua would assist him with paperwork during the evenings after his farming responsibilities were completed."

"Is that how my parents began their relationship?"

"It took several years for them to slowly grow fond of each other. I think my grandmother was the match maker. They were becoming partners and Joshua sincerely respected Abigail for her intellect, her devotion to reading and study. He overlooked her deficiencies in the domesticate arts.

After their marriage, your father continued the law firm when your grandfather left for Washington to serve as senator. He built up and impressive array of clients in his own right.

Of course, you were terribly spoiled. You were an only child. Your parents and grandparents doted on you. I am afraid it was your grandfather who spoiled you the most. His only son and other grandsons showed no interest in college or continuing the family law practice."

"I have fond memories of Grandpa. He helped me with my Latin and Greek, played chess with me. He spent hours talking about politics and the economy. He told me stories about far-away places. He inspired me to become a journalist, and to travel. I was not content to hear of these events second hand. I wanted to witness them for myself."

"You have done well. However, as a young man your education exceeded your wisdom," Jacob chided.

"Yes, I can see that clearly now. My family was a threat to my independence and to my ambitions," Thaddeus conceded.

"Only in your mind. Your parents were humble, hardworking people. Losing both in that accident was…" he stopped and stared out the window. "Here comes Rachel."

"I just learned about the excursion to Philadelphia. When do we leave?" She asked as she took a seat.

"We?" her father questioned.

"This would be a once in a lifetime opportunity – a business trip to view the latest inventions and to order new inventory. I will pay for my expenses after all, it is a business trip. Have you purchased train tickets? What are you waiting for?"

XV

1876 Centennial Exhibition

The Miller family gathered at the train station to see the party off.

Becky hugged her mother, "Have a wonderful time."

"I feel like a schoolgirl," Julia laughed.

Jonathon assured his father-in-law, "The boys and I will take good care of the farm, sir."

"I have no doubt you will."

"Peter, I wish you were coming with me," Rachel slipped her arm through his as they walked to the approaching train.

"I do too. I trust you will select the right merchandise for us to sell."

"I promise I will write and telegraph you often. This is an opportunity of a lifetime."

"Isaac, can you imagine a man my age taking his first train ride? We live in amazing times."

"We sure do. Pa, it is good to see you happy."

Thaddeus stood aside and observed the scene. There was no one there to bid him farewell as the train came to a halt.

"Cousin Thaddeus!" He turned around to see Charlie waving his doll. "Goodbye."

Jacob took a window seat with Rachel and Thaddeus seated beside him. Initially he found the noise and smoke to be annoying. "How fast do you think we are going?

"I guess between twenty and thirty miles per hour." Thaddeus was an experienced traveler. "It depends upon the quality of the rails and the terrain. Out west where it is straight and flat, trains can run up to sixty miles per hour."

"I cannot even imagine that!" the elderly man shook his head.

"Papa, we will spend the night in Portland and then catch an early train to Boston," Rachel explained. "We will take an express line, nonstop directly to Philadelphia. We will sleep on the train."

"There are beds on a train?"

"They are called Pullman cars, sir. There are lower and upper berths attached to the wall with a curtain, for privacy. I find the rocking motion of the train puts me to sleep," Thaddeus added.

"We live in amazing times!"

Jacob was both excited and fatigued when the train finally arrived at Centennial Depot in Philadelphia delivering them directly across from the main entrance to the Exhibition.[1] "May I suggest we get settled in our hotel rooms, rest and eat before we begin our excursion?" Thaddeus asked. There were over two thousand hotels and boarding houses in the city and Thaddeus selected the United States Hotel with three hundred and twenty-four rooms.[2] The $4.00 per night fee included meals and the Millers intended to get their money's worth.

"This is much larger than the Oxford House!" Eli stared in wonder. "I do hope the food is good. You know I am spoiled for Julia is the best cook in Fryeburg."

His wife smiled and patted his arm, "It will be better because I will not have to cook and clean up. This will be a wonderful vacation!"

Rested and fed, Jacob was eager to begin his tour. "Papa, we will take a trolley to and from the fairgrounds."

"Nonsense! Why spend money when we can walk for free?"

"Pa, the grounds are over 280 acres. We will be doing plenty of walking and sightseeing this week. Let us spend our nickels and save our energy," Eli reasoned.

Jacob did not enjoy the crowded trolley ride. "How many people are at the fair?" he asked Thaddeus.

"The organizers expect over nine million."[3.]

"It feels like they are all here today!" Jacob could not even image nine thousand people, never mind nine million.

The family paid fifty cents per person for admission and purchased an official guidebook.

"We must note the locations of the comfort stations," Julia suggested as she looked over the map.

"What?" Eli asked.

"The Department of Public Comfort offers a convenient location to meet if we choose to attend separate exhibits, it has a general reception room, a ladies' parlor, a lunch counter, lavatories and other amenities,"[4.] Thaddeus explained.

"Let's visit the Agriculture Hall first," Eli eagerly suggested.

"It only makes sense to begin in the Main Exhibition Hall since it is right here. Why walk across the entire grounds to see the Agricultural Hall?" Rachel contradicted. "The Main Hall has exhibits from all over the country and the world. Pa will not have to walk so far."

"I will leave you to enjoy yourselves. I have some interviews to conduct. I will see you back at the hotel tonight," Thaddeus tipped his hat with a smile.

"That sounds reasonable," Jacob agreed.

"Dear, we will be here all week. There will be plenty of time to visit the Agricultural Exhibit," Julia reassured.

"Then it is settled," Rachel stated as she took her father's arm and headed to the massive building.

"It looks like a palace!" Eli gasped in amazement as he stared at the enormous structure of wood, glass, and iron. "If it looks this fancy on the outside, I wonder what it looks like on the inside?"

"Let's go in and see for ourselves," Julia said sweetly and as she took her husband's arm. They strolled past the German exhibit of pottery, cloth, clothing, and ivory; Norwegian exhibit of glassware, jewelry, silverware, and cod liver oil; Austrian exhibits of Bohemian glassware, amber, leather goods, and cloth. Eli was tempted to complain before they entered the Swiss Pavilion. Here was the most impressive display of Swiss clocks, watches, music boxes and scientific equipment.[4]

Julia observed her husband studying a particular silver pocket watch. "I think you should buy it," she whispered.

"Oh, it is an extravagance for a poor farmer like me. I have better things to spend my hard-earned money on."

The family stopped at the sight of a thirty-foot, ornamental marble structure of James W. Tufts, Artic Soda, Boston, Massachusetts.[5] "This is a soda fountain?" Rachel asked in disbelief.

"It looks like something that should be in a museum," Julia agreed.

"The sign says it has seventy-six syrup dispensers. I am quite thirsty and would enjoy sitting down for a while. I would like a root beer," Jacob settled the matter.

"I think we should order different fruit flavors every day," Julia suggested as she read the list.

Jacob took a sip of his soda and wrinkled his nose. "This does not taste like Kate's root beer. Her grandmother's recipe combined all spice, birch bark, coriander, juniper, ginger ale, ginger, wintergreen, dandelion root, sarsaparilla, and sassafras root. This is bubbly."

"Charles Hires, a pharmacist right here in Philadelphia, combined more than twenty-five herbs, berries and roots to flavor carbonated water,"[6] Rachel explained.

"But why is it bubbly?"

"It is carbonated water. They have machines which create carbon dioxide which makes the bubbles in the water and add syrup," Rachel explained.

"How do you know this?" Eli asked incredulously.

"I am a businesswoman. Peter and I discussed the possibility of installing a soda fountain, but the cost is prohibitive."

"I cannot imagine something like this is Fryeburg," her brother contradicted.

"Obviously, it would not look like this! It is the carbonating machine, syrups, and dispensers that we would purchase. Since we wish to promote Temperance in Fryeburg, I think it makes sense to sell nonalcoholic beverages. Perhaps the saloons would not be so busy, if they had some competition, an alternative drinking establishment. For now, I must be content to purchase Mr. Hire's dried version of this root blend. My customers can add water, sugar and yeast and leave it to ferment."

Jacob patted his daughter's hand. "Your mother would be so proud of you."

"The Temperance forces banned the sale of hard alcohol at the Exhibition. I believe Mr. Tuft will make a small fortune this year," she commented.

"I feel quite rested and ready to go. Shall we continue? My daughter the businesswoman may want to transact some business," Jacob stood up.

"The imported items are too expensive for most of my customers. I need to search for American products," she stated as they continued.

The men averted their eyes and quickly passed the glass case filled with Farcy & Oppenheim of Paris of fine French corsets while the women lingered.[7] However, they stopped and stared at the Russian exhibit of fur pelts and stuffed animals.[8]

"I have heard about tigers, but I never thought I would see a real tiger pelt," Eli marveled.

"Look at that bear! It looks so real."

"There are two exhibits I need to visit. I shall not be long. The three of you can sit and rest in the reception area. I will be there shortly," she headed for the Lalance and Grosjean Manufacturing Company of New York.[9] They were one of the first American companies to make porcelain enamel ware – a cheaper, lighter alternative to cast iron cookware. After admiring the mottled blue "agate ware", she discussed wholesale prices and shipping rates before taking a business card.

She quickly scanned the glassware at the American Glassware Exhibit[10] where several companies were displaying their wares. She decided that the New England Glassware Company from Massachusetts had merchandise stylish enough to entice Fryeburg homemakers, and reasonably price to appease their husbands. She took the business cards with promises she would telegraph an order when she returned home.

She found her family sitting in the reception area of the comfort station studying the guidebook. "Tomorrow, we visit the Machinery Exhibit," Jacob announced. "Now we will return to our hotel and eat a proper supper and get a good night's sleep."

---- ✳ ----

After another crowded trolley ride, they paid their 50 cents admission and headed to Machinery Hall.[11] "A typewriter!" Rachel exclaimed as she headed to the Remington typewriter exhibit.[12] "I have read about these. Peter and I believe we can sell several of these."

"Mercy, they sell for $125.00!" Jacob exclaimed.

"I am sure Attorney Hastings can afford one. Perhaps Fryeburg Academy might need one." She inquired about wholesale prices, shipping rates with promises to telegraph an order as she took some business cards. Each family decided to pay the 50 cents to have a letter typed – Rachel sent a letter to Peter, Eli and Julia sent one to Becky and family. Jacob sent one to Charlie.

"Dear Charlie,

This letter is printed on a machine called a typewriter. I cannot believe the incredible things I have seen since I have left Fryeburg. Yesterday I drank root beer with bubbles in it. I cannot wait to return home and tell you everything. Be a good boy. I miss you.

Your Devoted Grandfather,
Grandpa

As they passed the National Suspender Company[12] Jacob announced, "I want to buy Charlie a pair of suspenders with his name woven in."

"What a great idea!" Julia agreed. "Eli let's get you, Jonathan and the boys matching suspenders."

Jacob laughed, "Well, I will need one and purchase one for Isaac and Danny."

"I will purchase one for Peter and a dozen to sell." As they waited for their suspenders, father and son excitedly planned to visit the display of firearms by Colt, Smith & Wesson, and Remington. "Julia, come with me to look at the Howe sewing machines," Rachel invited her sister-in-law.

"Emily would love one of these. Just imagine all the sewing she could accomplish!"

"I want to visit the Singer Sewing Machine[13] building."

"Does Singer have its own building? I do not think the men would enjoy that."

"That is why they will stay here while we go. I understand that the Women's Pavilion is nearby."

They found Jacob and Eli staring at the George H. Corliss Engine[14] where Eli was reading the plaque. "This 40 -foot -tall steam engine sits on a 56- foot -wide platform Two cylinders spin a flywheel which measures 30 feet in diameter, weighs 56 tons and produces 1,400 horsepower."

"I read in the newspaper that President Ulysses S. Grant flipped the lever on opening day. This engine is providing power for all the machines in this building."[15] Eli explained.

Imagine someday we could have a sawing machine or a shoveling machine. Farming would be much easier if machines could do the heavy work," Jacob said wistfully.

"We are going to the Singer Sewing Machine Building and Women's Pavilion. Do you wish to join us, or do you prefer to stay here?"

"We will stay here," Eli said distractedly.

"We will meet you at the Comfort Station at noon," Rachel instructed as she and Julia quickly exited the massive building.

Rachel purchased six Singer sewing machines and dozens of sewing patterns with directions for delivery. The ladies headed to the Women's Pavilion where they spent hours admiring art, education, engineering, religion, fashion, and inventions created by women.

"What is this?" Rachel exclaimed so loudly that several people turned their heads and frowned their disapproval at such un-lady like behavior. She failed to notice them as she hurried to the 'Mrs. Potts' Cold Handle Double-Pointed Smoothing Iron'[16].

"Julia, what is the one chore which you detest?"

"Ironing clothes of course. After you heat the sad iron on the stove, the handle is much too hot to hold – even wrapping a cloth around it. If you wait until the handle cools to a more comfortable temperature, then the iron is not hot enough to iron the wrinkles."

"Exactly! And Mrs. Potts discovered the solution. Look, she invented a detachable, insulated handle. None of these irons have their own handles. Now, you can have three or four irons heating on the stove. When the iron in your hand cools down, you simply return it to the stove, detach the handle, attach it to the next iron, and continue. With points on both ends, you can iron in both directions at once."

"This is brilliant!" Julia enthusiastically agreed.

"I am going to purchase a dozen of these. Women can accomplish so much. It is a shame that we cannot vote," Rachel lamented.

"I would like to try an ice cream soda," Julia attempted to change the subject.

"It is almost noon, let's meet Eli and Papa."

They found the men at the firearm exhibit. "Papa, let's share a chocolate ice cream soda," Rachel suggested.

"I have had ice cream and yesterday I drank one of those bubbly sodas. Why would anyone put ice cream in a soda?" Jacob shook his head.

"Let's have one and find out! I just ordered six Singer Sewing Machines. I know I can sell one to Danny for Emily. Once the ladies hear about Emily's machine, I am confident that the other five machines will be purchased as well."

"The other four," Eli corrected. "I am purchasing one for Julia. She and Becky cannot keep up with making clothes for five growing grandchildren."

"Eli!" she squeezed his arm in excitement. "But it is so expensive."

"It is an investment, like a new horse," Eli reasoned.

"Wisely stated," Jacob nodded his approval.

They ordered a chocolate ice cream soda with two straws. "What is this?" Jacob asked.

"It is a paper straw. You use it like this," Rachel demonstrated.

"What will they think of next," he shook his head and took a big sip. "This is good. I never tasted anything like this before! Do you think our hotel sells ice cream sodas?" Jacob asked with child-like excitement. "Charlie must have one of these. We must have a soda fountain in Fryeburg."

Eli winked at Julia as they sipped a strawberry ice cream soda. "I believe I can walk back to the hotel. I have had quite enough of those dreadful trolleys. Yes. A walk, one of those fancy suppers, another walk, another ice cream soda and early to bed for me! We live in amazing times."

❋

The next morning, Thaddeus joined the family as they planned to walk directly to the Agricultural building, but they were distracted by the imposing sight of the 300-foot-tall Sawyer Observatory.[17] "Just think of the grand view we would see up there!" Rachel grabbed her father's arm.

"How are we going to get up there?" Jacob asked incredulously.

"We will take the elevator.," Thaddeus explained.

"I read about these, but I never thought I would have to opportunity to ride in one," Julia added excitedly. "Oh, Eli, what an adventure!"

"Whoa! How do these thing work?" he stared at the car made of iron and wood with glass windows large enough to accommodate thirty passengers.

"It is hoisted up those long cables by a 40-horsepower engine," Thaddeus explained.

"I wish Charlie was here with me." Jacob headed to the line of passengers awaiting their turn.

Eli was speechless as the car slowly climbed upwards. Julia's eyes sparkled with delight as she hugged his arm. Jacob was as excited as a schoolboy. "How I wish Charlie was here!"

This is the largest structure in America," Thaddeus stated.

At the top they surveyed the entire fairgrounds, the city of Philadelphia and the surrounding countryside. "To think my father lived in that big city."

"I am sure Philadelphia was not that large ninety years ago," Rachel explained.

"For a farm boy from isolated Fryeburg, it must have seemed huge."

Eli remained speechless. "What do you think, Eli?" Julia asked her husband.

"I think we live in amazing times!"

Eli did not think anything else could compare to this experience until they strolled through the Kansas and Colorado buildings. Taxidermist, Martha Maxwell displayed 500 mammals and birds of the plains and mountains posed by a mountain and a stream[18].

"They look so real!" Julia gasped. The family stood and stared.

"I would like to take Jonathon and the boys out west and go hunting," Eli said more to himself. "What an experience that would be!"

"And why not? If I can take a train to Philadelphia, you can certainly take one out west," Jacob encouraged his hardworking son.

They finally made their way to the Agricultural Hall where father and son stood in front of the McCormick Harvesting Machine made in Chicago.[19] "I wonder how much one of these costs?" Jacob stated in awe.

"Too much for a small farmer like me. A machine like this would be very practical for the large farms out in the Mid-west that are flat, and treeless."

"We live in amazing times!" Jacob muttered as they headed to the displays of farming implements.

"Why don't you two plan to spend the day here while we visit some of the other buildings? We will meet you back at the hotel," Julia suggested with newly found confidence.

"Are you sure?" Eli asked.

"You have waited for days to visit this hall and I think you should spend as much time as you wish. Rachel and I know our way around. We will see you at supper." With an air of independence, she took Rachel's arm and headed off.

The ladies' first stop was in front of Henry Mallard's Chocolate Manufacturing of New York where they each enjoyed a bonbon. "I cannot remember the last time I had this much fun," Julia laughed as she took a second bite from the decadent chocolate.

"If we keep this up, we will need to loosen out corsets," Rachel giggled.

"Rachel, I believe it would be a very wise business decision to invest in chocolate," Julia recommended.

"I concur. Follow me to the Whitman booth." Stephan Whitman, a Quaker from Philadelphia, opened a confectionary and fruit shop near the city's waterfront. He was the first to package chocolates in printed, marked boxes.[20] "Boxes are much easier to ship and to display on shelves."

"Are you going to sell boxes of chocolates at your store?"

"Indeed. I will order a dozen."

"You should make it two dozen!"

"Two dozen it is!"

"We live in amazing times!" the ladies laughed.

❋

"The train is coming!" Charlie pointed excitedly as he stood up in Uncle Peter's wagon. "Do you see them? Do you see them yet?" he asked as the train stopped and the first of the passengers stepped down.

"There they are!" Peter smiled broadly as he and Charlie jumped down.

"Grandpa! Grandpa! Did you miss me?"

"I sure did Charlie. I have lots of stories to tell you! I drank soda with bubbles in it, took a ride in a glass box that went up as high as Stark Hill. I saw machines that sew, and machines that harvest plants. I took a trolley ride and a train ride. Do you know some trains have beds?"

"Grandpa, We live in amazing times!"

XVI

Autumn of '76

The arrival of the typewriters caused quite a stir in town. Peter demonstrated how it worked and allowed a few potential customers to test it out. Attorney Hastings announced, "I will take one. Please put it on my account and deliver it to me tomorrow."

When word spread that Attorney Hastings bought the first typing machine, several businessmen stopped in for a demonstration.

The Whitman boxes of chocolates were sold out within two days.

Charlie accompanied Uncle Peter to the train station to pick up six heavy crates. "Your Aunt Rachel will be thrilled when she sees these." There was a crowd waiting in the store, and several men offered to help unload the wagon.

"How does it work?" several women asked as they admired the new Singer sewing machines.

"Return tomorrow morning and I will demonstrate." Ever the shrewd businesswoman, Rachel knew there would be a crowd at her door the next day. She spent the rest of that afternoon displaying the new dress patterns, sewing notions, and fabric in a prominent location. She placed "Sold" signs on two of the crates and placed one near the display to demonstrate.

A dozen ladies watched the demonstration, before each taking a turn. Daniel arrived to purchase Emily's sewing machine. "It is a surprise," he explained. "She tires so easily after the accident. I thought this would encourage her to continue her sewing ministry."

"This is an investment for any lady who would like to become a professional seamstress," Rachel began. "Customers can select the desired sewing pattern and fabric," she pointed to the new display, "and a new dress can be made within hours."

Many disappointed ladies settled for buying a new sewing pattern. That evening several households debated the cost and reasons for purchasing a sewing machine. At the behest of a few irate husbands, Reverend Stone preached on the sin of covetousness that Sunday morning.

Daniel, Thaddeus, and Mr. Bennett enjoyed their pot of tea by the warmth of the stove in the family parlor on this cold and windy November evening. Mr. Bennett was continuously amazed by the Miller clan. Daniel was a wise, self-educated man who read literature, some of his grandfather's law books, some of his brother's medical books, and of course his beloved Bible. He was well-versed in most topics.

Sitting in this very room was a highly respected journalist, Thaddeus Pierce, who covered war stories in the Crimea and the War Between the States, violent revolutions in Europe, the tragic Potato Famine in Ireland, and the lawless Gold Rush in

California. He witnessed the Gettysburg Address, the funeral of Abraham Lincoln, and interviewed several Presidential candidates. Now he was living at Daniel's house through the winter while he wrote a biography of Karl Marx.

"Mr. Pierce, how did you become a journalist?" Mr. Bennett asked.

"My grandfather was the biggest influence on my life."

"Do you mean Senator Miller?"

"I was too young to remember him as a senator. I remember the elder statesmen from whom people from afar would seek his advice. He was a wise and kind grandfather who taught me everything I knew. We discussed the law and politics for hours. I had no intentions of following in his footsteps, nor hearing secondhand accounts of the momentous events in this country and abroad. Grandpa was content to discuss ideas; I wanted to meet the people who proposed those ideas. His personal recommendation opened the door to Harvard University when I was merely fifteen. I surely miss him."

"I miss him particularly around election time," Daniel continued. "Grandpa was simply livid when Andrew Jackson won over his friend, John Quincy Adams back in 1828. He would discuss each presidential candidate, their political platforms, their integrity, or the lack thereof."

"Who do you think your grandfather would vote for in this election?" Mr. Bennett asked.

"He was first a Federalist, then a Whig. He died before the formation of the Republican Party. I believe it is safe to say, he would never vote for a Democrat," Daniel laughed.

"I have interviewed both candidates, and I must admit that I am impressed with neither of the gentlemen," Thaddeus reported.

"There is a difference between impressive and integrity," Daniel contradicted. "Look how impressive war hero, General Ulysses S. Grant, was eight years ago. Yet his administration has been marked by scandals."

"Please tell us of your impressions of the two presidential candidates." Mr. Bennett had met numerous literary people through family contacts but did not personally know any politicians.

"Last year an overwhelming majority of both Republicans and Democrats in the House of Representatives voted against the principle of a third term[1]. Rutherford B. Hayes is not well known, but Danny, I am sure you would approve of him. He was a Union officer wounded several times while leading his troops in battle. A native of Ohio, he graduated from Kenyon College, then Harvard Law School, became a lawyer, and eventually the Governor of Ohio. He is the model of a Victorian gentleman and respectability. Rachel would approve of his wife Lucy who is a teetotaler."[2]

"What are your impressions of his opponent, Democrat Samuel J. Tilden?" Although Daniel knew he would be voting for the Republican Hayes, he did want to know more about the other candidate.

"Mr. Tilden is currently the Governor of New York. He lived his entire life in the state, graduating from law school, and having a very successful career in law with many wealthy, corporate clients including several of the railroads. He was a strong partisan of Martin Van Buren in state politics and a member of the Free -Soil Party."[3]

When Benjamin Miller was alive, Election Day was a family holiday, where the entire clan shared the noon day meal. Now it was an ordinary day where the men adjusted their schedule to visit the Fryeburg Town House in Center Fryeburg to cast their votes.

Thanksgiving came and passed, but no winner had yet been declared.

XVII

Hero of the Ice Harvest

It was a cold, Saturday afternoon in December, when Daniel, Emily, Mrs. Chase, Jeremy, and Mr. Bennett were eating their lunch in the kitchen by the warmth of the cookstove. The kitchen door swung open, and in walked Charlie dressed in wool overcoat, hat, scarf, and mittens and rosy cheeks.

"Mama says I am getting into too much mischief. I said I want to watch Uncle Eli finish building his icehouse. Mama says I would be a nuisance. So, I told her that I was going to Uncle Danny's house and be a nuisance!" he declared.

"I could take a break from correcting Latin translations. Perhaps, Charlie, you would be so kind as to escort me to your uncle's," Mr. Bennett offered. "I have never seen an icehouse before. The ice man would simply arrive at our door with his wagon and deliver the block of ice to our icebox in the kitchen."

"That is certainly more convenient," Jeremy acknowledged. "Most people who live in the Village do have their ice delivered. Many outlying farms that have access to ice, build their own icehouses and harvest their own ice."

"Sir," Mr. Bennett addressed Daniel, "both you and Dr. Miller have your ice delivered. Could not Mr. Miller have his ice delivered to his farm as well?"

"He did until this winter. My brother cannot remain idle during the winter. He thought this was a good time for Jonathan and him to build a large icehouse, recruit a few family members, and harvest some ice. Lovewell Pond is large enough for many families to harvest. Eli barters free labor from the relatives in the winter, and the relatives have free ice in the summer. Not only will he be saving money, but he will also be making money when Isaac and I and others purchase our ice from him."

"It is cold and back breaking work, but the families enjoy meals and fellowship for a several days. Winters can be long and isolating. The women enjoy their time together talking and preparing meals while the men spend the day competing who is the strongest and the fastest," Mrs. Chase chuckled.

This was not Mr. Bennett's idea of a good time. "Mrs. Chase, thank you once again for a delicious lunch. Charlie, I shall put on my winter apparel, and we will learn how to build an icehouse."

"I just want to watch. I don't want to learn anything!" Charlie grumbled.

"Uncle! Uncle!" Charlie called as they approached the building site. "I am here to help."

Eli, his son-in-law Jonathan, and youngest grandson greeted them with smiles. "We can use all the help we can get, Mr. Bennett," Jonathan invited.

"Have you ever built anything?" Eli asked the young instructor skeptically.

"Not exactly. However, I am here to assist in any way that I can. Or I can stay out of your way and watch and learn," Mr. Bennett offered.

"We are not stupid. Hayley says I am not stupid, and I can help. Mr. Bennett is smart – very, very smart!" Charlie volunteered.

"Mr. Miller…"

Eli interrupted, "Mr. Miller is my father. Call me Eli."

"Yes, sir. Please call me Emerson. Eli, how does an icehouse differ from a storage shed?"

"Good question. Right now, this 18' x 20' building is merely a shed. Some large, commercial icehouses can hold 80,000 tons of ice.[1] Today, we are building a second wall inside, and insulating the space between the two with hay and sawdust. When we stack the ice inside, we will insulate it with more sawdust to reduce melting."

"You have plenty of sawdust!" Charlie added.

"Why don't you two boys fill the wagon with hay and sawdust while the three of us erect the inner walls," Eli instructed his ten-year-old grandson, Eddie, and Charlie.

"Yes, Grampy!" the two younger boys eagerly scampered off to the barn.

"It will take them all day to fill that wagon," Emerson pointed out.

Jonathan laughed. "That's the idea. They are not in our way, nor are they are in the house disturbing the ladies, and Charlie can spend the afternoon playing with his cousin."

"We have spent the morning cutting the boards. Emerson, you would be a big help if you will hand us the boards and then hold them in place while we nail them."

Emerson was relieved to be assigned to a job which he could do. "What made you decide to become a farmer?"

Eli stared at him. "I am the fourth generation of Millers to be a farmer. What else would I be? Julia is a farmer's daughter. Jonathan is a third-generation farmer and he and Becky will take over the farm when I'm gone."

"Emerson is not a name you hear of every day. Is it a family name?" Jonathan asked.

"Actually, I am named after Ralph Waldo Emerson," he boasted. When the two farmers showed no sign of recognition, he explained "Ralph Waldo Emerson is a well-known poet, speaker, and abolitionist. He also lives in my hometown of Concord, Massachusetts, and was a close friend of my father." There was no response as the two men continued pounding nails.

Twenty minutes later Eli volunteered, "My grandfather was an abolitionist. My father could tell you stories about the Underground Railroad. My brother, Danny, took on the family avocation when he owned the lumber mill by the Saco until the War Between the States."

"You Millers are quite the family!"

"I am just a farmer," he shrugged. "Can you check on the boys and see if they have any hay and sawdust in the wagon? We can begin to insulate this wall."

Emerson entered the barn where Eddie was dropping hay from the hayloft into the wagon below. "Where's Charlie?"

"He went to the house to get us some doughnuts," he replied as he began climbing down the loft.

"I knew that my mother would not give me the doughnuts, but she would never turn down Charlie. Mr. Bennett, have you ever milked a cow?" he asked with an impish grin.

"I never had the pleasure."

"It's not hard. I can show you," he offered.

"Well, I don't know if I should," he deferred.

Eddie grabbed a bucket and a three-legged stool, and headed to the large black bovine with its head secured and contently eating hay. "Have a seat," he grinned.

Emerson took the offered bucket and sat on the stool. One quick survey of the animal's anatomy revealed this was no cow! The boy burst into laughter just before the bull kicked Emerson off the stool.

Charlie witnessed the scene as he returned with a handful of doughnuts. "You are a sinner! You are a very big sinner! You know Mr. Bennett is not cow smart!"

"What is all that yelling?" Eli stopped his work.

"Whatever it is, it doesn't sound good," Jonathan headed to the barn where he found Emerson moaning on the floor, holding his left shoulder.

Charlie was yelling, "Now my father has to cut his arms off, and it's all your fault! You are mean. You are very mean, and you are not my cousin anymore!"

"Edward, get in the house! I will deal with you later," Jonathan said with gritted teeth as he helped Emerson to his feet.

"Charlie and I will take Emerson to see my brother, while you go inside to handle family matters," Eli suggested after surveying the situation.

To Emerson's relief, Isaac's waiting room was empty when the good doctor asked, "What happened to you?"

"He tried to milk a bull and the bull didn't like it! Mr. Bennett is not cow smart. Do you have to saw his arms off?" Charlie asked.

"Well, let's see," Isaac stifled a laugh.

"No broken bones. I will not need to amputate," Isaac announced. "You may have fractured your collar bone." After a shot a morphine and his arm carefully placed in a sling, the humiliated patient was taken home.

Eli paid the bill and telegraphed Mrs. Bennett that her son would not be visiting for Christmas. Three days later the icehouse was completed.

———❋———

In January, Daniel and Charlie had volunteered to take Emerson to and from the Academy and carry his books for the next six weeks. One sunny Friday afternoon, Charlie excitedly ran into Mr. Bennett's office. "Uncle Danny is taking us to watch them scribe the ice. Hurry up before it gets dark!" Charlie grabbed the books off the desk, "Hurry."

Daniel helped Emerson into the carriage. It felt painstakingly slow as the horse lumbered down Bradley Street, turned left onto Pine Street, then down another road which led to Lovewell's Pond.

"They already cleared off the snow!" Charlie pointed out as the wagon came to a stop. Eli's cousins and nephews from the Wiley and Frye families were still shoveling.

"What is Eli doing?" Emerson pointed to the farmer walking behind his horse.

"That is called an ice plough. See how it scribes lines in the ice?" Daniel explained.

"Yes, the ice looks like a checkerboard with horizontal and vertical lines. Why are they doing that?"

"This ensures each block of ice is of uniform size."

"These blocks will be huge. How will they possibly get them into the back of a wagon?"

"We will come back tomorrow, and you will see! Will you come with me?" Charlie invited.

"I was planning to …"

"Please! Summer and Hayley don't want to go, and Papa will be busy with sick people. Mama won't let me go by myself. Jeremy can't watch me because he is going to be a pike man."

Emerson had no idea what a pike man was, nor did he wish to spend an entire day standing in the bitter cold and wind.

"Please! You are not very ice smart. You could learn a lot."

Emerson remembered how some of the students took great pride helping with the ice harvests. This would be a step in getting to know his students better as well as making Charlie happy. "I have schoolwork to do in the morning. How about I pick you up after lunch tomorrow?"

"I am the luckiest boy in the whole world!"

Charlie was warmly dressed and waiting as Mr. Bennett arrived. "You look like Uncle Danny!"

The young teacher nodded as Summer asked. "Are you wearing Uncle Danny's great coat?"

"Mrs. Miller insisted. I am also wearing one of Jeremy's wool hats and socks. Mrs. Miller knitted this scarf for me last night. I did not argue for I knew I would not win," Emerson laughed.

"It is a good thing. Your city boy clothes wouldn't keep you warm," Mahayla added.

"Mahayla!" Summer gasped in exasperation.

"Miss Miller, that is an astute observation. My occupational endeavors keep me indoors. I have much to learn from these

Fryeburg men beginning with their wardrobe. I am sure I will be most grateful for this attire as we walk to the pond."

"Charlie, do not be a nuisance!" Lydia reminded. "Mr. Bennett, if he misbehaves, take him home right away."

Charlie chattered excitedly through their half hour walk, down McNeil Street[2], then the road by the large Warren Tannery. Once they crossed Portland Street unto Pine Street, Mr. Bennett recognized where he was.

"Mr. Bennett, you are smart, very smart. Don't listen to what those mean boys say about you. They say mean things about me too. Uncle Danny says to forgive them. It's because you and I are different. You and your books, and city boy clothes, and your fancy words. Half the time we don't even understand what you're saying. It's not bad to be different."

"Charlie, you are wise beyond your years." Emerson now realized perhaps he tried too hard to impress his students and their families. People may have mistaken his insecurities for arrogance.

Two large horses pulling a wagon loaded high with blocks of ice approach. "Mr. Wiley!" Charlie waved.

He stopped, "Charlie did you come to help?"

"No sir, I promised to watch from shore and not be a nuisance."

"Mr. Bennett, how's the arm? Heard about your accident."

"I think I need to spend less time in a book and more time in a barn," he replied.

"Be happy to teach you anything you want to know. Me and the Mrs. will have you over for Sunday dinner sometime."

"That is most kind. I will look forward to it."

"Well, there's an icehouse waiting to be filled." With a tip of his hat and a shake of the reins, Mr. Wiley headed up the road. His two sons and a nephew were waiting as he backed the wagon up to the icehouse. Two of the men set up a wooden ramp up to the wagon as Mr. Wiley and the third man pushed the blocks with ice tongs.

"The next wagon should be here soon," Mr. Wiley instructed as he left the younger men to carefully place the blocks and insulate them with sawdust. Once the wagon was safely beyond the farm, Eddie quietly left his hiding spot behind a large pine tree, hopped onto the back of the wagon, and hid under a piece of burlap. A quarter mile before the frozen pond, Eddie jumped off the wagon and ran into the woods.

As they finally reached Lovewell Pond, Emerson was indeed grateful to the two caring ladies who insisted he dress warmly. "Looks like the men have accomplished a great deal this morning."

"First, they used their long ice saws and cut the ice following the scribe lines. Jeremy says it is very important for the first few blocks to be cut perfect. See how they made a channel of open water? This is very important because all the other blocks will travel down the channel. See Jeremy using the pike to push the blocks down the channel? Those pikes are heavy, and the metal tips are sharp, very sharp. I am not allowed to touch them." Charlie felt proud to be teaching Mr. Bennett.

"Maybe in a few years when your bigger and stronger you can help," Mr. Bennett suggested.

"Do you think so? Do you really, really think so? I couldn't bring Charlie Doll with me. It would not be safe for him," he looked down at his much-loved doll held in his right hand.

"This certainly looks like dangerous work. You would be wise to leave Charlie Doll home with your family."

"Or you could watch him. He is very quiet and would not disturb you while you are reading your big books. Plus, he likes you very, very much," he added with his crooked grin. "See, once the block is at the end of the channel, the men use those large ice tongs and slide it up the wooden ramp to the back of the wagon. You have to be strong, very, very strong to do that job."

"Charlie, you are extremely ice smart," Emerson complimented. Mr. Wiley returned with his empty wagon. "Now you can see how they use the ice tongs." When his wagon was filled, they could hear another wagon approaching.

Emerson admired the teamwork and precision of these self-sufficient men. Although not afraid of hard work, they still enjoyed themselves as they joked and laughed. Once Jeremy took a break and came over to greet them. He seemed genuinely pleased to see his teacher had come.

"This is most impressive. Charlie has been explaining each job preformed. He is a very good teacher. This has been very educational," Emerson complimented.

After a five-minute visit Jeremy turned, "Gotta get back to work. Maybe next year you can join us," he invited.

Because all the men were facing the shore as they worked, and Emerson was focused on them, only Charlie spied Eddie in the distance boldly walking across the ice. He was tempted to tell Jonathan that his youngest son was on the pond, but he knew it was bad to tattle.

Eddie enjoyed his hard-won freedom sliding along the ice with a cold wind in his face. He was not concerned about safety because he knew the ice was at least thirteen inches thick.

However, unbeknownst to him, some men had a cut a channel on Friday, before deciding to relocate to the other side of the pond. Overnight a thin layer of ice had covered the open water. He fell through the ice gasping as he was engulfed by the freezing water.

"No!" Charlie screamed as he threw his doll on the snow, running and sliding across the pond.

"Charlie!" Emerson followed and fell on the ice.

"Mr. Bennett, are you hurt?" Jeremy came walking over.

Ignoring the searing pain in his left shoulder he commanded, "Get Charlie! He is running across the pond."

Jeremy and Jonathan put down their tools, chased, and called for Charlie to come back.

"That boy belongs in one of those schools for imbeciles," one of the Frye cousins muttered.

Charlie continued running and sliding until the opening of the ice. "Eddie! Eddie!" he laid down and stuck both arms in the freezing water, grabbing his cousin's collar to keep his head above water.

"Help! Help! I can't get Eddie out of the water!" Charlie yelled as Jonathan and Jeremy approached.

"Eddie? Eddie!" Jonathan yelled. The other men began running over. "Bring the ice gaff!" he commanded. Jonathan and Jeremy were struggling to pull him out.

Eli arrived with the others. Jonathan grabbed the gaff and caught Eddie's collar with the curved hook. As he slowly and carefully began to lift his son out of the water, the other men grabbed the child's arms and lifted him upon the ice.

Mr. Wiley appeared with his wagon minutes before the men returned to the shoreline with the two young boys. Jonathan had taken off Eddie's wet clothes and covered him with his own winter coat. Jeremy took off Charlie's coat and mittens and dressed him in his jacket and mittens. The four of them seated themselves in the back of the wagon. Eli helped Emerson up to the driver's bench, sat down, took the reins and the horses went galloping to the Isaac's office.

Emily and Mrs. Chase made a fuss over Emerson, as he returned home under the influence of another shot of morphine and a new sling. As he drank his second cup of tea, he and Jeremy relayed the harrowing experience.

"This indeed has been a day to remember," Emerson slowly rose to his feet. "If you will excuse me, I think I shall retire early this evening." Mr. Bennett would be wearing his sling for an additional four weeks.

Both boys were sent to their beds. That night Charlie developed a cough and a fever. Isaac found Mahayla reading to her brother when he came to take his son's temperature. "Charlie Doll is not sick because he stayed on shore, but he was scared, very, very scared."

"I would be scared too," his father agreed. "You were very brave today."

"I'm not stupid. I am brave."

By Sunday afternoon half the village heard of the incident.

When Reverend Stone came for a visit Charlie informed him, "You should go visit Eddie. He is a very big sinner."

"The Bible says we are all sinners, Charlie," the good pastor reminded.

"Some are bigger sinners than others!"

The last week of February, Emerson telegraphed the Portland Daily Press suggesting the paper write an article on Charlie's heroism. Four days later a journalist and a photographer arrived in Fryeburg by train. They interviewed all the witnesses of the rescue. Jonathon repeatedly told the reporter if it had not been for Charlie, not only would Eddie have drowned, but the family would also have had no idea where he was. Eli recounted Charlie's illness and his inability to return to school and the day he ran for help when his aunt had fallen down the stairs. Finally, the photographer set up the large awkward camera in Isaac's front parlor. Charlie, dressed in his Sunday best, patiently posed for the photograph.

On Tuesday, March 7, 1877, the Portland Daily Press printed the heroic tale on page 4. The front page was devoted to photos and articles on the inauguration of Rutherford B. Hayes as the 19th President of the United States. President Hayes was declared the winner of November's election just a few days before the inauguration.[2]

Charlie kept a copy of the newspaper for the rest of his life.

XVIII

The New Church

Sunday morning of June 3,1877 Summer, Mahayla, Charlie, and Charlie Doll entered church late. Isaac was called out on an emergency, and Lydia was in bed with a headache. They tried to inconspicuously slip into the pew behind Uncle Danny. At the close of the third hymn the organist returned to his seat and the pastor climbed the stairs to the pulpit.

"That is not Reverend Stone!" Charlie objected. "Where is Reverend Stone?" he ignored his sisters' attempts to quiet him down. "Is he sick? Did he die?" Charlie grew more agitated. "He's a stranger!" he pointed to the scowling man dressed in a black robe standing at the pulpit. "I want Reverend Stone!"

"Madam," the pastor address Mahayla, "if you are incapable of controlling this incorrigible child, I will ask you to leave."

"This is my church! You are a stranger! You cannot tell me to leave," Charlie defied.

Uncle Danny stood up, and wordlessly escorted his nephew down the aisle with a mortified Summer and an indignant Mahayla trailing behind.

Once outside Uncle Daniel instructed, "Please do not disturb your mother."

Charlie muttered to himself as the three of them dejectedly walked toward home. "Look! That is Reverend Stone's carriage," he pointed to the vehicle parked in front of the Oxford House and began running. Reaching the hotel well before his sisters, he entered the building following the sounds of singing to the large meeting room. Owner Asa Pike built this room where the Oxford County Superior Court held its fall hearings. There was Reverend Stone, Dr. Towle, Mr. Alonzo Lewis and more than a hundred and fifty men, women, and children.[1] They were having church – a new church. He and Charlie Doll stood in the back of the room staring at the scene in disbelief.

Later that afternoon Charlie and his sisters were invited to have tea in Uncle Danny's front parlor. "Charlie, do you know what my job is at the church?"

"You visit sick and poor people. Aunt Emily makes clothes for the people at the poor house. You bring them clothes and visit them. Everybody knows that."

"That is correct. I am a church elder. Another part of my job is to ensure that the Word of God is preached correctly. Over the past several months, the elders and Reverend Stone have been discussing some of his changing views on the Bible. He felt it was time to preach what he truly believed. We felt we could not allow him to preach those beliefs, which are contrary to Scripture."[2]

"You fired Reverend Stone?" Mahayla asked.

"Most certainly not. We mutually agreed it was time for him to go his separate way. Charlie, I was wrong not to tell you this before you went to church this morning. I had no idea you would react this strongly."

"That stranger called me a bad name in front of everybody."

"Reverend Mason is a very good man, but he was wrong to call you a name."

"Can I still be friends with Reverend Stone and Mr. Lewis?"

"People with different ideas can be friends."

Thaddeus knocked on Emerson's door. "Would you care to join me for the Inquisition?" he joked.

"I beg your pardon?"

"Danny invited Reverend Stone and Alonzo Lewis here to discuss their 'heresies' with Charlie and the girls. We and Jeremy are invited. Plus Mrs. Chase baked an apple pie."

"This sounds like an evening well spent."

Two dining room tables were pushed together, guests were cordially greeted, and everyone sat down to enjoy their dessert.

Daniel began the discussion. "Charlie, do you know what Freedom of Religion means?"

"It means we are free to go to church."

"It also means we are free not to go to church," Thaddeus added.

"Both of you are correct. It means that people are free to worship God in different ways, have different beliefs, and go to different churches."

"Can people in different churches still be friends?" Charlie asked.

"Of course, they can. We will always be friends," Reverend Stone reassured.

"Charlie, I am leaving next week for Europe. When I return home in a few months I will invite you and your family over and tell you all about it," Mr. Lewis explained.

"Next week, I am going to your church!" Charlie declared to his uncle's chagrin.

"You should go to church with your family," Reverend Stone said kindly.

"Don't I have Freedom of Religion?" Charlie challenged.

Thaddeus snickered. "Not in this family!"

"You don't go to any church," Charlie argued. "Why can't I go to the new church?"

"Freedom of Religion is for grownups. Your family should go to church together. When you are a grownup, you can decide what church to go to," Reverend Stone calmly explained. "Then you can decide what you believe."

"I know what I believe, The Bible is the Word of God, and it is true. Don't you believe that?"

Reverend Stone hesitated and looked to Daniel for guidance. "My views on the Bible have evolved over time. I don't believe we must take everything in the Bible literally, that the stories in the Bible depict deeper spiritual realities within us." [3.]

Daniel continued, "We noticed Mr. Stone excluded all references to the Trinity and the Christ's atoning of our sins on the cross. At first, I was not concerned about what he preached, but what he chose on not to preach. Gradually over the next three years I feared he was straying from our Orthodox Congregational views. However, a few weeks ago a visiting Methodist minister approached the elders stating that he clearly recognized several of Emanuel Swedenborg's teaching in Mr. Stone's sermon. [4]

"I have never heard of Emmanuel Swedenborg. Who is he?" Mr. Bennett asked now deeply interested in the conversation. Baman Stone's eyes lit up at the opportunity to share his newfound faith. "Emannuel Swedenborg was born in the late 1600's in Sweden to a highly respected Lutheran minister. He was an extremely intelligent and well-educated young man, and a member of the Royal Academy of Sciences.

In 1745 he gave up his worldly science to devote fulltime to the study of the Scriptures and Hebrew. During this period, he had full communication with angels and had visions of the spiritual world. He believed that nature corresponds to a reality of the spiritual world. This knowledge of correspondence is necessary to understand the heavenly secrets of the Bible. He felt a divine commission to write and publish these new truths and to convince the world of the soundness of these doctrines. He never intended to leave the Lutheran church, but to illuminate it. Ralph Waldo Emerson held his doctrines in high esteem," [5.] he nodded to Mr. Bennett.

Emerson joined in, "It is the natural progression for the church to evolve from the Pilgrims to the Congregational Church to Unitarian."

"Actually, that is a historically inaccurate statement," Thaddeus contradicted. "The Pilgrims, who arrived in 1620 on the Mayflower were Separatists. They wanted to totally separate themselves from the corrupt Church of England. On the other hand, the Puritans, who arrived in Boston in 1630 on the Arabella did not wish to leave the Church of England, but to purify it. Over the decades they formed the Congregational Church where there was no church hierarchy, and each congregation was an independent entity.

In 1794 Joseph Priestly arrived from England introducing his beliefs in Unitarianism, which denies the Trinity. It appears that the clergy ignored these 'heresies' until a Unitarian was appointed a Chair at Harvard Divinity School. By then it was too late. Unitarianism had infiltrated the churches."[6] Thaddeus

Pierce may not have been a religious man, but he certainly was an educated one.

Turning to Emerson Bennett, "Now let's talk about your First Parish Church back in Concord. Reverend Emerson was the Congregational pastor of this great church. I believe he was the grandfather of your highly esteemed friend, Ralph Waldo Emerson. Upon his death, Reverend Ezra Ripley accepted the position, moved into the parsonage, and married Widow Emerson. Gradually over the decades, he preached Unitarianism until the numbers of Unitarians exceeded the numbers of the Congregationalists and they took over the church. The displaced Congregationalist then built the Trinitarian Church in town."[7]

"What is the difference between a Unitarian and a Universalist?" Daniel asked. His cousin never failed to surprise him.

"That is simple. A Universalist believes God is too good to send man to hell. A Unitarian believes that man is too good to go to hell," he laughed.

Charlie did not understand the conversation. "Do you believe in Easter? Do you believe that Jesus died on the cross for our sins and came alive on Easter? That is my favorite Bible story." Thaddeus envied Charlie's child-like faith. When did he lose his?

"I believe that God is Love and Wisdom and not capable of judgment, punishment, or anger. The Bible is a symbolic story of our inner lives and speaks to us on many levels. It is our call to be vessels of this love, and to share it, whatever form it may take. It is not about accepting any doctrines, but rather on leading a life of love." [8.]

"Can I have another piece of pie?" Charlie had enough theology for one evening.

"Sir, have you read the writing of Ralph Waldo Emerson and Henry David Thoreau? Are you also a transcendentalist?" Emerson asked excitedly. He finally met someone in Fryeburg who understood!

The minister shook his head. "Emerson was a philosopher, not a preacher. Transcendentalism is a reaction to intellectualism. His followers were seeking spiritual experiences by transcending the material world of reason. Thoreau turned to nature for his spiritual solace. It is a philosophy which begins with man and ends with man."

Charlie yawned loudly. Mr. Lewis laughed, "I think that is our cue to say good night."

"When I realized that my preaching was causing divisions in the church, I decided to leave the congregation and begin a new church. It was never my intent to take over the church as many before me have done. Mr. Miller, I thank you for your hospitality and your continued friendship. You may invite me over anytime Mrs. Chase serves apple pie," Mr. Stone laughed. "Mr. Bennett, you are welcome to attend our services anytime."

The Miller clan, like many Fryeburg families, was divided about the "church question". Eli, who was disillusioned with church after the tragic death of his son, decided he and Julia would attend the Church of the New Jerusalem. Jonathon, Becky and their five children joined them. Emerson decided to visit the new church while Thaddeus continued to stay home. Daniel and Emily attended the Congregational Church as usual.

As Lydia prepared breakfast for the family Mahayla defied, "I am never setting foot in that church again! I am an adult and I choose to exercise my right to Religious Freedom."

Isaac looked at his strong-willed daughter, and realized that the more he argued with her, the more determined she would become. Should he assert his parental authority? Danny insisted that faith was a personal matter, not an inheritance. "Very well. You are an adult free to make your own decisions, even if I should disagree."

There were more empty pews in the Congregational Church as Isaac's family, minus Mahayla took their seats beside Danny and Emily. After the hymn singing Reverence Mason climbed the stairs to the pulpit.

"Today, we shall begin a series on forgiveness. We are all born sinners and need the forgiveness of our Savior. Before we turn to the Scriptures, I must first ask for forgiveness for myself. Charlie Miller, I was wrong to lose my temper and berate you in front of the congregation last week."

"You are a sinner, a very big sinner," Charlie responded. The church filled with tension.

"Indeed, I am."

"I am not stupid. Hayley says I am not stupid. Grandpa says I am a blessing."

"Yes, Charlie you have been a blessing to many people over the years. I could learn much from you," the pastor humbly confessed.

"Do you believe in Easter?" Charlie asked suspiciously.

"Easter is the epitome of centuries of fulfilled prophesy. It is the culmination of Christ's atonement for our sins. If He did not rise from the dead, he would simply be another martyred prophet. But He is Son of God, the second in the Holy Trinity, our Savior, and the Forgiver of our sins. It is through His resurrection that we may have hope in our future resurrection at His Second Coming. Easter is the very foundation of our faith."

"That is good, very good. I forgive you. As long as you believe in Easter, I will stay in this church."

Mahayla and Jeremy took their seats beside Mr. Bennett and Dr. Towle. Both gentlemen could not hide their surprise. "I am exercising my rights to Religious Freedom," she declared.

Jeremy noticed Mahayla sounded just like her Aunt Rachel when she talked about women's right to vote. "I am curious, that's all," he confessed. "I cannot reject or believe in something that I do not know."

"Well said," Mr. Bennett approved.

XIX

Beginnings and Endings

Emerson assisted his mother and Lily step down from the train. "Your carriage awaits, my ladies," he grinned as he bowed.

"Really, Emerson," Mrs. Bennett scolded with exasperation. "Why on earth did you insist we attend another one of these dreadful commencements.?"

"It is lovely to see you too, Mother," he laughed. "And Lily, you look as lovely as always." He kissed her hand.

"What is this surprise you were hinting at in your letters?" she demanded crossly.

"It is the beginning of a new life," he stated mysteriously as he escorted them to Daniel's carriage.

"This is much better than that filthy wagon and those farm boys," Mrs. Bennett emphatically stated, as Emerson helped her into the carriage.

"What exactly do you mean by the beginning of a new life?" Lily insisted.

"Everyone will hear tomorrow. All I can tell you is I will no longer be an instructor at Fryeburg Academy," he teased.

"Emerson, you are impossible!"

"I trust you will enjoy your accommodations at the Oxford. I have made dinner reservations this evening for us."

Sunday afternoon Mahayla was getting dressed for her commencement. "Mother, please do not fuss with my hair. I like pulling my hair back in a ribbon."

"Charlie Doll likes your hair the way it is," her brother added.

"Lydia, I agree with Charlie Doll. Her hair looks fine." Isaac winked at his son.

"Jeremy likes her hair that way," Summer stated.

Lydia put down the brush and went downstairs in time to answer the back door. "Hello Eli. Do you need more chairs for the party?"

"The boys and I will start setting up soon. Pa is having one of his spells. Julia and I would feel better if Isaac could check in on him before he leaves for commencement."

"I heard that," Isaac called as he and Charlie came down the back stairs. Tell Pa, I will grab my bag and be on my way over."

"Tell Grandpa I will grab Charlie Doll and we will be on our way over."

The doctor and his faithful assistant found Jacob fully dressed but laying on top of his bed.

"I am just having one of my spells. I should be good as new after a rest. I do not want you to be late for commencement."

Isaac opened his black bag and took out his stethoscope. "Let me listen to your heart and then we will be off. He carefully listened to a weak and irregular heartbeat.

Beginnings and Endings

"I want to listen too." Charlie smiled at the sound. "Grandpa don't worry. You are alive."

"Eli, I do not think we should leave him alone while we go to Danny's to set up," Julia voiced her concern.

"Aunt Julia, he will not be alone. I will be here," Charlie offered.

"We don't want you to miss Mahayla's graduation," she argued.

"I don't like the mean ladies with the pretty dresses. I will stay with Grandpa."

"Yes, we don't like those mean ladies with the pretty dresses," Jacob agreed. "Charlie and Charlie Doll will stay with me. He can run next door to fetch one of you if he needs to. But you need to get ready for the party."

"Grandpa, would you like me to tell you a story from the olden days?

"Charlie, we are leaving you in charge," Isaac packed up his bag.

"Leave the stethoscope," Jacob instructed.

Charlie listened to the beating heart. "He is still alive."

Eli laughed. "I can see Pa is in good hands. Let us head out."

Emerson picked up the ladies at the Oxford and brought them to the Academy early. They selected two seats in the last row hoping to avoid the Millers. Twenty minutes later Isaac, Lydia and Summer arrived, politely waved to them, and found seats near the front. The auditorium filled quickly, and the graduates took their seats on stage. Reverend Mason opened with a benediction. Three speeches later, the diplomas were distributed. Finally, the Director of the Board of Trustees stood up to address the audience.

"As some of you may have heard, our Headmaster, John Fiske, is leaving his post at the close of this school year. Our search committee has reviewed and interviewed several fine candidates, and selected a truly outstanding man. He is committed to the pursuit of truth and knowledge. He is both liked and respected by his students, parents, and peers. He is diligent and humble. I know you will all be as pleased as I am to learn our next Headmaster is Mr. Emerson James Bennett."

The audience loud applause muffled the sounds of Lily's comments. "Emerson cannot be serious! This is not happening."

"I am honored and humbled to accept this position. I believe I have learned more from my students than what they have learned from me."

"Like milking a cow!" someone heckled.

He laughed good naturedly. "I have learned the difference between a cow and a bull and have the scars to prove it! We all learn from our mistakes. Learning is a two-way street. My wise friend Charlie told me, 'Mr. Bennett you may be book smart, but you are not cow smart.' Every member of the Academy and the Fryeburg community has wisdom and knowledge to acquire and to impart. I hope to continue the academic excellence and moral training of our young people. May Fryeburg Academy continue to be the institution of which we may all be proud. Thank you."

He received handshakes and congratulations for over a half hour. "You will make an outstanding Headmaster," Isaac shook his hand. "Will the three of you be attending Mahayla's ice cream social this afternoon?"

"I do thank you for the invitation. I believe Mother made reservations for afternoon tea at the Oxford." He strained his neck searching for them in the crowd.

"They left to get some air," Summer politely informed him. He found the distraught women waiting for him in Daniel's carriage. "Emerson, really. How could you?"

"I did it for us, Lily. It is a very distinguished position with a reasonable salary and a lovely home. Think of the fun you and Mother will have furnishing the house. You shall be an elegant hostess for ladies' teas and receptions. Would you like to see our house? You can spend the summer planning our wedding and selecting furniture."

"Emerson, you cannot be serious. I could never plan a proper wedding in two months. What would people think of me?"

"Perhaps the two of you can discuss this privately in the gardens back at the hotel?" his mother suggested as she nodded at the numerous by standers milling around.

As the three of them slowly headed down Main Street, many pedestrians waved and shouted their congratulations. Upon arrival at the Oxford House Mrs. Bennett headed upstairs to change her outfit, leaving the couple to meander to the back garden. They silently sat on a bench staring west at the White Mountains.

Emerson broke the silence. "I thought this is what you wanted–a gracious home, the status of being the Headmaster wife, serving as hostess. I thought you would be pleased. I do not understand. What is wrong Lily?"

"What is wrong? I thought I was marrying into a family of high standing. I thought I would spend the rest of my life being a lady of a fine home, spending time with my friends and family, entertaining the best and the brightest New England has to offer. I thought our children would be raised in a proper home and not in some farming community milking cows. Whatever possessed you to try to milk a cow?"

"It turned out to be a bull," he corrected. "I wanted them to like me. I wanted to be one of them."

"Well, you are not one of them. Go back to the Board of Trustees and tell them you have changed your mind."

"Perhaps I am more like them than you realize. I am accepting this offer. The matter has been settled."

"You will be returning in August alone, for I shan't marry you." She stood up.

"Lily, wait!" he pleaded.

"I have made my decision. I will never marry you." Picking up her skirts she quickly walked away. He sat on the bench staring straight ahead.

The Miller family converged in the backyard at Daniel's house where several make-shift tables and benches were set up. Mrs. Chase had baked an apple spice cake, and Julia, Becky and her children made chocolate, and vanilla ice cream.

Rachel proudly made "Temperance Punch" the day before. This recipe simply required the juice of twelve lemons and six oranges plus thinly peeled zest, two cups of boiled cranberries, copious amounts of sugar and water.[1] Although the new First Lady, Mrs. Rutherford B. Hayes, a temperate woman was often ridiculed as "Lemonade Lucy",[2] Rachel held her in high esteem.

Holding a plate of cake and ice cream in one hand and a glass of punch in the other, Mahayla took a seat beside her Uncle Peter. "Well young lady what plans to you have in store?" he asked already knowing the answer.

"Jeremy and I are ready to begin our apothecary by the middle of this summer. I need to purchase a scale just like the one you use and would like you to order dozens of tins, bottles, and corks. We will pay cash, for we do not wish to begin our business in debt."

"That is wise, young lady. Beware your aunt will try to sell you a typewriter," he joked.

"Ma, did you hear that Mr. Bennett is the new headmaster?" Jeremy asked excitedly.

"I wonder if this means he will be moving out to live in the headmaster's house," Mrs. Chase mused. "The boys will certainly miss him."

"I had not thought of that," he replied glumly.

"Lydia, I am going to check in on Pa," Isaac stated as he finished his last spoonful of chocolate ice cream.

"Please send Charlie back here to the party. He probably has talked your father's ear off."

As Isaac entered the kitchen he heard, "Oh no! There is no heartbeat. He must be dead. Grandpa! Grandpa!" Isaac ran down the hall and heard his father's response. "Charlie, dolls do not have hearts. They live by imagination."

With a sigh of relief, he entered his father's bedroom. "How is the patient?" he asked as he observed his father's gray pallor and slight blue tinge around his lips. Charlie moved the stethoscope from the doll to his grandfather.

"Yup, he is alive."

"Let me take a listen to concur." The heartbeat was much slower and erratic. He could hear a crackling sound in his father's lungs accompanied by shallow breathing. "You are correct. He is indeed alive. I think it is time for you to eat some cake and ice cream. Run to the party and ask Uncle Eli to join us."

"I will leave Charlie Doll with you, Grandpa, so you won't miss me."

"Aunt Julia, can I have some ice cream? Papa wants Uncle Eli to come."

"Mrs. Chase will get you some ice cream and I will go find Uncle Eli."

Eli and Julia tentatively entered Jacob's room. "Pa?" Eli asked failing to mask his concern.

Jacob slowly opened his eyes. "I was just telling Kate what a wonderful time we had in Philadelphia. We should go again next week."

"Pa?"

Isaac intervened. "Pa, there is something I want to tell you and Eli – as a doctor, not as a son. You are dying, Pa. Your heart is growing tired, and it is slowing down. There is nothing to fear. It will not hurt."

"Of course, there is nothing to fear," he whispered. "For the Lord is my Hope and Salvation."

"Father Miller, would you like me to get Danny and Rachel?"

"Is Rachel at the textile mill?"

"She is at Mahayla's graduation party. I will be happy to get them," Julia rushed out of the room holding back tears.

Rachel and Daniel found four dining room chairs set around their father's bed and took a seat. "Papa?" Rachel took her father's hand.

He smiled at the sound of her voice and slowly opened his eyes. "Rachel, my dear girl," he whispered. "Have you sold many typewriters?"

She nervously laughed. "A few."

"Spending time with you at the Exhibition was one of the best times of my life. Remember our chocolate ice cream soda? Your mother would have added a little mint." He took a deep breath and closed his eyes.

Beginnings and Endings

"How long does he have?" Daniel whispered to Isaac.

"Hard to tell. Hours. Maybe days. I read that hearing is the last of the senses to go. You should all talk to him. I am sure he can hear."

"Of course, I can. I am not deaf."

"Pa, thank you for teaching me everything I know about farming. I promise I will take good care of the farm."

"Remember what I told you. There are some things more important than farming."

"Yes, sir."

"Listen to your brother."

"Which one?" Eli asked.

"I meant Danny," he clarified. "Danny, take care of your brothers and sister for me. They will need you. You are just like your grandmother, Hannah."

"Thank you. She taught me everything I know about the Bible."

Jacob took a deep breath and exhaled.

The siblings would spend the entire night together.

---❋---

Wishing to avoid the Miller celebration, Emerson took the carriage to Conway and found a peaceful spot by Conway Lake to review the day's events. He was experiencing mixed emotions of excitement, hurt, rejection and relief. "It is for the best," he told himself. After a few hours, he headed back home certain that the party would have ended, and he could quietly return to his room.

As he led the horse to the stable, he observed the party had ended rather abruptly. There were dirty plates and silverware strewn on the various tables. He collected the dirty dishes and entered the kitchen where he found the three Mrs. Millers and Mrs. Chase sitting glumly around the table.

"Mercy, I forgot all about them!" Mrs. Chase blushed.

"Is anything wrong?" he looked around.

"Father Miller is dying," Lydia said sadly. "His children have been with him all evening. His grandchildren have gone in to say goodbye. Tomorrow we shall schedule a vigil. I am sure there are many people who would like to pay him one last visit."

As word spread of Jacob's impending demise, church members, fellow farmers and two dozen nieces and nephews streamed in and out of the old farmhouse sharing food and stories. Charlie made daily house calls with the stethoscope. On Thursday afternoon Charlie announced, "Charlie Doll wants to stay with you tonight and keep you company."

Jacob quietly looked at this much-loved grandson and whispered, "You are a blessing."

That evening Isaac returned to the farm with this black bag. "I need a few minutes with my patient," he explained to his siblings and nodded to the bedroom door to emphasize his request. After they reluctantly left, he closed the door, placed his bag on the floor and sat on his father's bed.

"Pa, can you hear me?" he whispered.

Jacob opened his eyes and nodded.

"I have some family secrets to tell you. I promised I would never tell, but I knew you would understand. Davy was a deserter. I forged his discharged papers. I knew it was wrong, but I did it anyway."

Jacob reached for his son's hand and squeezed it.

"The day before he died, he told me he had found an abandoned dying Confederate soldier screaming in agony. He shot him to put him out of his misery. I told him to pray and ask for forgiveness and God would forgive him."

Jacob nodded his head in approval.

"But Davy could not forget or forgive himself. He hung himself in the barn that night. Eli and I found him, and we made it look like an accident. Eli wanted to protect Julia and the family from the truth. Eli does not know about the discharge papers or the Confederate soldier. It is my fault, Pa. I should not have left Davy alone after he told me."

Jacob opened his eyes. "This was not your fault. The secret killed him. No more secrets. Get your brothers and sister."

"Pa?"

"We must tell them of the letter."

Isaac opened the door and invited them back in. "Pa has something to tell you."

"Papa, what is wrong?" Rachel took her father's hand.

"I have a secret to tell my children," he gasped for breath. "Isaac, tell them about the letter."

"What letter?" Eli demanded.

"Is this the letter Ma told Aunt Harriet about?" Daniel questioned.

"When Pa was a young boy, he was writing at Grandpa's desk and needed a sheet of paper. While he was looking in the top drawer, he found a legal document. It was a sale's receipt for a purchase of a slave in Philadelphia."

"I do not believe one word of this. Isaac, he is delirious," Rachel objected.

"I do not believe it either," Eli agreed. "Grandpa was an abolitionist. Why would he buy a slave?"

"To legally move her out of Philadelphia and to Fryeburg. He had to buy her before he could marry her," Isaac quietly explained.

"Marry her? What are you talking about?" Eli demanded.

"Grandpa bought Nana, brought her to Fryeburg to marry her," Daniel explained. "Nana told me herself, after Grandpa died. She did not want me to stop working for the Underground Railroad just because Grandpa was gone. She made me promise not to tell anyone."

"Your dear mother found the letter years ago and told Aunt Harriet. She loved me anyway," Jacob whispered. "Now I can die in peace."

"But how was Nana a slave?" Eli still could not believe what he was hearing.

"Because she was a Negro," Isaac explained in exasperation.

"I have met many light-skinned Negroes. Quadroons have three white grandparents and one Negro grandparent. Octoroons have seven white great grandparents and one Negro great grandparent. I am guessing by her lighter complexion, she was an octoroon," Daniel explained.

"That explains our dark curly hair," Rachel muttered.

"Are you telling me, we are Negroes?" Eli asked in disbelief. "My children are Negroes?"

"We are all God's children. The Lord does not divide us by race; man does," Daniel continued.

"We have fifteen white great, great grandparents and one Negro great, great grandparent. I guess that just makes us Americans," Isaac declared. "I think my patient and Charlie Doll need some rest."

Beginnings and Endings

The four of them silently kept vigil.

When Charlie awoke Friday morning, he found Charlie Doll in bed beside him.

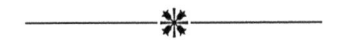

---❄︎---

On Monday afternoon Emerson took a seat with Jeremy and Mrs. Chase, while the Millers sat in front of the crowded Congregational church. Reverend Mason had graciously asked Rev. Stone to give the eulogy. "Jacob Freeman Miller did not own a book; yet he was one of the wisest men I know. He was a man of few words, yet his actions spoke volumes.

Because he believed that all men were created equal, he participated in the Underground Railroad with his family. He displayed no partiality. He treated everyone, from politicians to the oppressed, with equal respect. Because he was a devoted husband and father, his family never went without. He taught all four children the value of hard work by his example. He suffered many losses within his lifetime, his beloved parents, his only sister, and brother-in-law, two grandsons and most recently his dear wife. He grieved without becoming bitter. He was not a wealthy man, yet we will all be the poorer now he is gone."

As the congregation stood to sing *My Hope is Built on Nothing Less*, Emerson wondered if he would ever have a family who would mourn his passing. Would people remember him for his wisdom or for his book collection? Would Lily's rejection make him bitter, or would he continue his new life with the same fortitude as Mr. Miller?

Over two hundred people entered the new Pine Grove Cemetery where he would be buried with his beloved Kate, but not his parents and grandparents. They were buried in the old village cemetery behind the stone school. Emerson stood in the back observing it all. Farmers, shop keepers, Attorney Hastings, the postmaster, Dr. Lamson, many of Isaac's patients, Mahayla's classmates, one friendly train conductor, a tanner, numerous members of the Frye, Wiley and Walker clans, and many regular customers at Evan's General Store. The crowd listened to Pastor Mason's benediction as his three sons and son-in-law slowly lowered the simple pine casket into the grave. As the crowd dispersed, Emerson quietly followed the Millers as they converged at Daniel's house.

The younger Millers congregated outside while the four siblings, their spouses and Mrs. Chase sat in the dining room quietly talking. "Emerson, please join us," Daniel invited. "Congratulations on becoming headmaster."

"I do not wish to intrude."

"Not at all. You are part of the family," Emily explained.

"First thing tomorrow morning Jonathan, the boys and I will begin planting." Eli was clearly distraught.

"That is exactly what your father would want you to do," Julia reassured her husband.

"Tomorrow morning, I will be meeting a new business owner. I believe she wishes to purchase a scale and a quantity of tins, bottles, and corks. I know both my parents would be so proud of Mahayla," Rachel stated teary-eyed.

"I will pull out the old apothecary wagon from the stable and get it ready for the road. They cannot limit their business to Fryeburg. They must expand their markets," Daniel contributed.

"Spoken as a true businessman," Peter approved.

Isaac turned to Emerson and explained, "When I returned home from the war, but before I became a doctor, my mother and

I began a travelling apothecary. Lydia and I traveled throughout Maine and New Hampshire selling our herbal remedies."

"Isaac, I will not allow our daughter to…"

"I should say not!" Mrs. Chase agreed. "Jeremy is capable of traveling alone while Mahayla remains here working in the gardens and resupplying the inventory." The two mothers agreed.

"Of course, you would need to only make initial contacts and sales. Additional orders can be sent by telegram and shipped by train. That is how the store orders and receives some of our merchandise," Rachel explained.

"We live in amazing times. Look at all the changes within our father's lifetime," Daniel declared.

"What are your plans, Mr. Bennett?" Emily asked.

"I will go to the Academy and pack up my old office and meet with Headmaster Fiske to begin our transition. May I continue to board here? I have grown fond of the company I keep here and do not relish living in an unfurnished house alone."

"We would love to have you!" Mrs. Chase invited.

"Mrs. Chase is correct, we would enjoy having you live here as long as you wish," Daniel confirmed. They were too polite to ask about Lily.

"Dr. Miller!" a neighbor came running in the back door. "Excuse me, Charlie said I would find you here. The Osgood boy fell out of a tree. His mother is rather distraught. She thinks he broke his arm."

"I am on my way."

XX

Mr. Peary

~~~~~~~~~~

"Here comes the train," Charlie excitedly pointed to the oncoming locomotive to Jeremy. They watched the train come to a stop and many passengers exit the cars. "There he is! Who is he talking to?"

"Emerson Bennett? Is that you? What are you doing here?"

"I am the headmaster at Fryeburg Academy. I live here. Robert Peary, what are you doing here?"

"Emerson, please allow me to introduce you to my mother. I have not found an engineering job after graduating from Bowdoin. Mother has relatives in the area, and we have rented a house in Fryeburg."

"Mr. Bennett!" Charlie stood in the wagon waving Charlie Doll in the air. "Over here, Mr. Bennett!"

"Do you need a ride to the house? There is plenty of room in the back of the wagon for our trunks." Mr. Bennett offered as the three of them headed to the empty wagon.

"Robert, Mrs. Peary, these are my two friends, Jeremy Chase, and Charlie Miller. Jeremy just graduated from the Academy and helps run the boarding house in which I am currently living.

Mr. Peary

He has plans to open his own apothecary and Charlie is one of my literature students."

"We read *Twenty Thousand Leagues Under the Sea*. I help Jeremy and Hayley in the herb garden. I am going to work in the apothecary too."

"Mr. Peary and I attended Bowdoin together, although I was two years ahead. He and his mother will be living in Fryeburg."

"Is this your first visit to Fryeburg," Jeremy politely asked.

"Mercy, no. I have relations in Fryeburg and have been visiting the area for years. I am a member of the Wiley clan," Mrs. Peary explained.

"My Nana was a Wiley. She married my Grandpa, Jacob Miller. She died. Aunt Harriet died too. Thank heavens. We thought she would outlive us all!"

Mr. Peary stifled a chuckle as the heavily loaded wagon slowly lumbered to McNeil Street.[1.] They stopped in front of a newly built, two story, white house with three gables.[2.] "Thankfully, it is furnished, and we only brought the necessities."

"I do have several more trunks due to arrive later this week," he reminded his mother. "Jeremy, may I hire you to pick up the trunks and deliver them here?"

"We will do it for free. Any friend of Mr. Bennett's, is a friend of ours." Charlie assured the newcomer.

The trees were in peak foliage when Mr. Peary entered Evan's General Store one October afternoon. He had never seen before the sides of mountains splashed with patches of spots of crimson and yellow relieved by the dark green of the pines and firs.[3.] The town may not be the most exciting place for an ambitious young man to live, but it certainly was one of the most beautiful. "Well hello Charlie. What are you doing here? Should you not be in school?"

"I work here for Aunt Rachel and Uncle Peter. School is a very mean place. Charlie Doll and I did not like it there. May I help you find something, sir?"

"I hope so. I need some paper and pencils. I also need three more oil lamps and a few quarts of kerosene."

"Kerosene is good, very good. It comes from the ground. Whale oil comes from dead whales. That is very bad."

"Charlie, I never thought about it that way, but I believe you are correct. If I pay for my purchases now, would it be possible to have the lamps and kerosene delivered?" he asked as he placed two silver dollars on the counter.

"Uncle Peter and I will deliver them at the end of the day. Hayley does not need me in the garden now. I keep Uncle Peter company, so he does not get lonely. Plus, I know where you live."

Mr. Peary smiled. "Very well then. I will be expecting you and Mr. Evans later this afternoon. Good day," he tipped his hat and held the door open for a beautiful young woman with red hair.

"Hello Charlie. Good afternoon, Aunt Rachel," Summer greeted.

"Is this a social visit or are you shopping?" Rachel asked.

"Perhaps a little of both. Papa says I may purchase a fountain pen and put it on his account."

"You have a fountain pen," Charlie argued.

"Yes, I have an old fashion pen where I must continually dip in the ink well. It is most irksome. I would like to purchase one of the new pens with an ink reservoir. I am beginning a new novel and Papa says I must have a Cross pen like his."

"Could we perhaps convince him of the necessity of owning a typewriter?" Rachel slyly asked.

"I tried. We are compromising on a new pen."

"Oh no!" Charlie groaned. "I forgot to give Mr. Peary his change. May I run down the street to his house and give it to him?"

"Yes, you may. But walk do not run. You must not overexert yourself."

Charlie grabbed the change and his jacket, and briskly walked out the door. He enjoyed his ten minutes of freedom, for he was not often allowed to walk by himself. He proudly walked up to the Peary's front door and knocked.

"Well, hello Charlie. What a pleasant surprise!" Mrs. Peary greeted.

"Good afternoon, mam. Is Mr. Peary available? I forgot to give him some money back."

"He is in his work room upstairs. Follow me," she invited. "Bertie, you have a visitor," she cheerfully announced as they entered.

His work room was a sanctuary from boredom and anxiety about his future. He found the views of nature from his window to be a source of wonder. He could look eastward to a range of low, hazy mountains and southwestward across a grassy field and then dense woods and to Starks Mountain, steep, tree covered rise. He was determined to explore all those areas.[4.]

Charlie looked around the room in amazement. "Mr. Peary, I have your change." He handed over the coins.

"Well, that was very thoughtful of you. You could have returned it with your delivery."

"Mr. Peary?" he began tentatively. "I do not wish to alarm you, but your owls are dead, sir." He pointed to two specimens standing on a table.

The young man tried not to laugh. "I am a taxidermist," he explained.

"A what?"

"A taxidermist. I take dead animals and preserve them. See? Here are two owls[5.] and I am working on a pheasant."

"That is strange, very, very strange. Do you preserve chickens?"

"I am afraid that there is not much demand for chickens."

"Good. Chickens are bad. This is very, very strange," he muttered as he descended the stairs and left through the front door.

Two days later Mr. Peary spied Charlie and the beautiful redhead approaching the house. He opened the door to greet them. "Charlie, it is good to see you again. To what do I owe this pleasure?"

"Sir, I am Summer Miller, Charlie's sister and I am here to invite Mrs. Peary to Sunday afternoon tea at three o'clock at my aunt's house."

Mrs. Peary appeared behind her son. "That does sound delightful."

"Ladies only? No gentlemen?" Mr. Peary protested.

"I think Mr. Bennett and Uncle Danny would enjoy your visit. Please do come," Summer invited.

"And Jeremy and me." Charlie added.

"We shall be delighted," Mrs. Peary accepted.

Summer, Mahayla, and Lydia helped Mrs. Chase prepare the finger sandwiches, scones and tea and set the tables in the dining room. Both Jeremy and Charlie were dressed in their Sunday best.

Daniel greeted his guests, "We are so pleased the two of you were able to make it today."

Mr. Bennett entered the foyer. "Robert, I hear I have you to thank for this invitation. I think you will enjoy the company of the Miller ladies."

"Emerson, how are things at the Academy?"

The men headed to the dining room. "You have a lovely home, Mrs. Miller," Mrs. Peary complimented.

"It is only this quiet on weekends when our boarders return to their homes," Emily laughed. They entered the dining room. "This is Mrs. Chase. Harriet is like a daughter to me, and I do not know how I ever managed this house before she came.

I believe you have met my nephew Charlie and niece Summer. This is their sister Mahayla, and their mother Lydia. Dr. Miller is out on a house call and will try to visit later."

Mr. Bennett hoped it was not too obvious when he pulled out a chair for Summer and took the seat beside her. The younger people sat at one table while the older adults took seats at the other table.

"Both Summer and Mahayla were students of mine before they graduated."

"What are you ladies doing now?" Mr. Peary asked.

Charlie answered, "Hayley, Jeremy and I raised herbs in Nana's garden. Hayley and Jeremy make medicines from them. When we have enough, we will open our own apothecary. Summer is going to be a famous writer."

"Charlie, it is not polite to interrupt. Do you want to sit at Mama's table?" Summer scolded. Charlie scowled, and wished he had not left Charlie Doll at home.

"Summer was one of my most gifted writers. I am sure she will be quite successful in whatever she may choose," Mr. Bennett complimented.

"I plan to become a doctor. The apothecary is a means to earn money for my education," Mahayla explained.

"How interesting," Mr. Peary nodded.

"Mr. Bennett is my teacher too!" Charlie interrupted. "He reads me stories like *Tom Sawyer* and *Swiss Family Robinson*. I like *Black Beauty* the best. I like horses. I help Jeremy take care of his horse. Horses are good, very good."

"After Charlie's illness, he found it difficult to return to school. We have our own school for him," Mahayla explained. "We work in the herb garden together in the mornings and then he works at the General Store in the afternoon. Some evenings Mr. Bennett comes over to read to Charlie."

"That sounds fascinating. Charlie, would you like to help me draw a map of Fryeburg?" Mr. Peary offered. "Every morning we can walk back and forth, stepping out the distances of the village. In the evening I will do the figuring necessitated by my surveys during the day. When the surveying is done, I will begin the work of drawing the actual plan."[6.]

"Will there be dead birds looking at me?" he asked suspiciously.

"No. My taxidermy work is a means to earn money while I am working on my survey. That is a separate job," he reassured.

"Did you study map making in college, Mr. Peary?" Summer asked.

"I studied Civil Engineering.[5] However, there were no offers of promising positions for civil engineers, no openings or leads into the future. Mother and I decided to move to Fryeburg.[7] It is only until something better comes along."

"I arrived over two years ago with the intention of staying until something better came along. However, I discovered everything I need or want is right here in Fryeburg," Emerson declared.

"Charlie, I will pick you up tomorrow morning at eight o'clock sharp."

Charlie was so excited; he could hardly sleep. His father had torn out a few pages of college notes from an old leather journal and presented it with two pencils the night before. He was up before sunrise and found Summer sitting at the kitchen table writing and drinking coffee. "I like to write early in the morning while it is still quiet," she explained.

"Will you keep Charlie Doll company today? I cannot carry him and my journal and pencil," he explained. What he did not say was he did not want Mr. Peary think he was a baby.

"Of course, I will. Shall I make us some breakfast."

"Thank you. You are a much better cook than Hayley."

There was a knock on the front door promptly at eight o'clock. Charlie ran to the door and found Mr. Peary wearing a large canvas rucksack on his back. "Can Charlie Doll come too? He can ride on your back."

"Well, if Charlie Doll can go to work with you at the store, there is no reason he cannot come with us on our journeys."

Lydia appeared with some bread, cheese, an apple, and a mason jar of water. "May I impose upon you to carry these?"

"Yes, mam. I brought some food and water as well."

"I can show you Grandpa's Farm."

"Not today. I have a plan. I want to complete Main Street first. Then you may select the first side street."

"Charlie, please be good," Lydia pleaded. "Mr. Peary, if he gives you any trouble, please send him home."

"Don't worry, Mama. I will be good."

She closed the door after them and whispered, "I hope so."

Most of the lots on Main Street in the village had houses or businesses. Charlie pointed to each house and named the occupants. "Good morning, Charlie."

"Mr. Peary, this is Uncle John. He is not my real uncle like Uncle Danny. Everybody calls him Uncle John. His real name his John Smith. He is a famous stagecoach driver and has the best horses in the world. Don't tell Uncle Eli I said that. He gave the town some of his property to build a street from the train station to the Oxford House.[6.] Everybody likes Uncle John!"

"Pleased to make your acquaintance," Mr. Smith shook the younger man's hand. "Beautiful morning to take a walk."

"Hello, Charlie. A good day to take a walk, Charlie." Every person they met greeted Charlie by name.

"Charlie, you have many friends."

"Those people are not my friends. They are only nice to me because I am famous. I am very, very famous. I had my photograph in the newspaper."

"That is quite impressive for a young man of your age. What did you do that made you famous?"

"I saved a little boy's life. The grownups were harvesting ice on Lovewell's Pond. He fell in the water and none of the grownups even noticed. I ran to the hole, screaming for help, laid down on the ice and stuck my hand in the water and grabbed him by his collar. The water was cold, very, very cold. Those people called me a simpleton before I was famous. Now they are nice to me. They are not my friends."

"That's an insightful observation for an eleven-year-old."

"This is the blacksmith shop. This is Dr. Lamson's house. He is a doctor and a telegraph man. If you want to send a telegram, you go to his house.[7.]

"You have to put this house on your map," Charlie ran to the kitchen door of a three-story white house and knocked with Mr. Peary reluctantly following behind.

"Mrs. Tarbox, this is my friend, Mr. Peary. He is smart, very smart and is making a map of Fryeburg. His mother is a Wiley. I think we should put your outhouse, which is inside your house, on his map."

Mr. Peary blushed but Mrs. Tarbox laughed. "That is fine. Charlie's Aunt Emily and I are part of the Walker clan. I have known Charlie all my life. We are practically cousins."

Charlie led the three of them to a former bedroom which had been converted to the "outhouse inside the house". "Mr. Seth Page installed this room. Mama wants Papa to hire Mr. Page to build one for our house. It has both hot and cold running water! You do not need to heat up water on the cookstove. See!" he demonstrated by turning the faucets. "You do your business right here," he pointed to a copper tinned tub inserted in a wooden frame with a flush. The tank was placed above. He pulled the chain which flushed the water out of the contraption. "Have you ever seen anything as wonderful as this? And look at the size of this bathtub!"[8.]

"Yes, I have, Charlie. I have visited a few homes in Portland with water closets."

"Portland is a long way to travel to do your business," Charlie shook his head.

The two adults laughed. "Mrs. Tarbox, you have been more than gracious."

"You and Charlie are welcome to visit any time."

"This is the church. It has a new clock in the steeple. Miss Sarah Osgood gave the church $200.00 to buy and install a clock."

"That was very nice of her," Mr. Peary complimented.

"Well, she's not going to use it. She's dead," he explained. "Dr. Lamson takes care of the clock."

"Dr. Lamson sounds like a busy man!"

The two of them continued down Main Street with Charlie chatting. "Mr. Lewis! Mr. Lewis! This is Mr. Peary. We are making a map of Fryeburg! Mr. Lewis is really my friend."

"Yes, Charlie and I are really friends," he chuckled. "Enjoy your map making."

The two of them continued down Main Street. "Charlie Doll is enjoying his walk today. But he wants to stop because we are thirsty."

They stopped at an empty lot with a westward view of the White Mountains[9.] to drink some water and to eat an apple. A carriage went racing by, running over a stray dog, but did not stop. The small brown dog yelped in pain, ran on three legs before collapsing at Charlie's feet.

"This is bad, very bad." He started crying and picked up the whimpering dog. "My father is a doctor. He can fix Charlie Dog. You go make your map. I will take care of Charlie Dog. That is more important."

Mr. Peary took the dog into his arms. "You are right. This is more important."

Mr. Peary

The waiting room was filled with patients. "Papa, I have an emergency!"

Isaac came running out of his office as Mahayla came running into the waiting room. "Charlie, I care for people, not dogs."

"Fine. Hayley and I will fix him. I will get the ether. Mr. Peary get the bone saw. Hayley knows how to amputate legs. You want to be a doctor. You can be a doctor today!" He gently took Charlie Dog away from Mr. Peary and carried it to the back office.

"Excuse me. I will be right back," Isaac apologized as he followed the three of them to the back office. "Charlie, get the hydrogen peroxide," Mahayla instructed. She studied the leg. It is not broken. Possibly fractured. We will clean out the wound so it does not get infected, and I will bandage it. Mr. Peary, please bring over those cloth bandages."

"Well, I see Mahayla has everything under control here, I will tend to my real patients," Isaac smiled with pride at his daughter.

Charlie petted the dog's head and spoke softly to it. "Don't be scared, Charlie Dog. I am going to take good care of you. I will give you food and water and a straw bed. Charlie Doll and I will never leave you. Mr. Peary, I am sorry I cannot spend the rest of the morning with you."

He took Charlie Doll out of the rucksack and handed it to Charlie. "I understand. This is more important."

———✷———

That evening Mr. Bennett stopped by the house with a copy of *Around the World in Eighty Days*. "I am sorry, Mr. Bennett, but Charlie is in the stable with his dog. Mother will not let the animal in the house, and Charlie refuses to leave its side," Summer explained.

"Perhaps, I may spend the evening with you. I am interested in hearing about your writing."

"Remember when you told me I needed to write about my experiences, and not someone else's? I believe that was good advice. I am writing about a little girl whose father is away at war, and her mother is not coping well. She tries so hard to be perfect, hoping to please her distraught mother. Life becomes more confusing for her when her injured father returns home. It is the story of the struggles of one soldier and his family to adjust to life after the battle at Gettysburg."

"When you are ready to show it to me, I would be honored to read it."

"Thank you for treating me seriously and not like some silly girl with unrealistic dreams. Thank you for telling me what was wrong with my first story. Thank you for challenging me to do better."

"I understand. My grandfather, father and uncle owned a successful publishing firm in Boston. My mother had high expectations of me carrying on the family business with my uncle, and to play an important role in society. After Father died, I tried everything to please her. Courting Lily was her idea, not mine. I knew after my first year of teaching here, this is where I belonged. I was never good enough for Lily or her father. I am grateful she broke off the relationship. I only wished I had the courage to break it off with her first."

"But you did not want to disappoint your mother," Summer smiled.

There was a knock on the front door. "Oh dear, I do hope it is not a patient," Summer mumbled as she headed to the door.

"Mr. Peary?"

"I came to visit Charlie Dog. How is he doing? Good evening, Emerson. Are you here to visit Charlie Dog as well?"

"No, I am here to visit Summer. You can find all three Charlies in the stable."

Two weeks later the three Charlies were ready to join Mr. Peary on his mapping expedition. Emerson continued to read to Charlie during the evenings.

It was a cold, clear January night when Emerson knocked on the back door. "Summer is not here. She took a walk with your friend Mr. Peary. The entire family went with him to the empty lot to look at the stars," Isaac informed him.

"Thank you, sir." He found the Millers including Charlie Doll and Charlie Dog listening to Mr. Peary.

"We are here to discover True North or Geographic North."

Emerson interrupted, "Robert, any compass will point you to the North."

"They are not the same thing. The magnetic north is the direction indicated by a freely suspended and balanced magnet. We are here to observe the North Star and to establish a meridian line here on this lot."[11.]

"What is a meridian line and why is it important?" Mahayla asked.

"The direction given by the acute angle between a line and a meridian is known as bearing True Meridian. The direction from any point along a meridian towards the North Pole of the earth is defined as true north. That is, the north according to the earth's axis. True meridian passes through the center of the north and south poles, but not necessarily, in case of magnetic meridians. When I am done with my calculations, I will mark my work by two posts. These will be used to correct compasses."[12.]

"Why not be satisfied with magnetic north and a compass?" Emerson asked. It appeared to be much work for nothing.

"It is absolutely necessary if one wishes to discover the exact location of the North Pole."

That Friday night dozens of young adults ice skated by the light of a full moon on a local pond. Mr. Bennett, with a paired of borrowed skates, and Jeremy stopped by to escort Summer and Mahayla to the skating party. A disgruntled Charlie whined he wanted to go too.

"Sorry, this evening is for your sisters to go out and have fun. We can play checkers," Lydia offered.

Charlie brightened. "Charlie Doll likes to play checkers."

The two couples found someone playing the fiddle while people skated, and others sat on benches warming themselves by the bon fire. "Look, there's Robert," Mr. Bennett pointed, and Summer waved to Mr. Peary inviting him over.

"Mr. Peary, how ingenious!" Summer complimented as he skated over with Clara Mason. He had rigged a chair with skates so the ailing young lady could join her friends for the evening.

"I am having a wonderful time!" Clara beamed.

"Everyone is," Mr. Peary smiled. "Hurry up and get your skates on!" he invited as he and Clara skated off.[13]

One beautiful spring morning Mr. Peary arrived on horseback. "Good morning, Charlie. Our morning walks are over. I thought we would celebrate with a ride up Jockey Cap."

"That is good, very, very good!" Charlie Doll was placed in Mr. Peary's rucksack with his head peeking out so he could enjoy the view and Charlie Dog happily trotting along.

Now Mr. Peary was busy drawing up his map, calculating his meridians, and expanding his taxidermy business. Charlie drew two copies of his own map. He proudly displayed one in his father's waiting room and the other in his bedroom. Charlie Dog was now allowed in the kitchen and Charlie's bedroom.

That summer Charlie, Hayley, and Jeremy spent every spare minute, increasing the size of the herb gardens. Summer continued to assist her mother with paperwork and to write. For the first time, Emerson did not return to Concord for the summer but worked in his office at the Academy.

The year of 1878 fell into a comfortable pattern. Charlie, now twelve years old, worked at the general store, most of the day. Uncle Peter let him hitch the horse to the wagon and drive to the train station under his watchful eye. Mahayla often ate supper with Jeremy at Uncle Daniel's house and spent the evening together making more salves and tinctures, and writing a business plan for their apothecary. Emerson visited with Summer each evening and read a chapter of literature to Charlie. Mrs. Peary occasionally invited the Miller ladies to tea, and Charlie would visit with Mr. Peary and watch his progress on the Village map.

Life changed dramatically for Mr. Peary during the spring of 1879.

Finally, the survey of Fryeburg was completed. It was the best piece of draftsmanship he had ever done. He was in good spirits when his mother asked him to walk to the post office to mail some letters where he spotted a notice tacked up on the wall. The Office of the Coast and Geodetic Survey in Washington needed more draftsmen. Applicants were requested to mail in samples of their work. Only six draftsmen were needed nationwide. He quickly returned home, wrote to the Coast Survey, sent his cherished plan of Fryeburg, and arranged to take the competitive examination.[14]

The day he received his acceptance letter he breathlessly rushed into the General Store. "Charlie! Charlie! I am leaving for Washington! I got the job!"

The day before Mr. Peary's departure, Charlie and Charlie dog stopped by to wish him well. "I have a present for you so you will not forget me."

"I could not forget you, Charlie," he responded as he opened the muslin bag and pulled out a copy of Charlie's map of Fryeburg in a wooden frame. "Thank you, I will keep this forever. I have a present for you as well." He handed him two stuffed owls. "They are Charlie Owl I and Charlie Owl II."

"That is ridiculous! Everyone knows that owls are not named Charlie. They are Oliver and Owen Owl."

"Will you be attending the reception for me tonight?"

Charlie shook his head. "Hayley and Jeremy, Summer and Mr. Bennett are going. But Mama says it is for grownups. Jeremy and I will give you a ride to the train station. I promise to give Oliver and Owen a good home. If you write me a letter, I will write you back."

"Promise?" Mr. Peary smiled.

"I promise."

XXI

Seeking

One January evening of 1880 after the students retired, Mr. Bennett discovered Thaddeus studying in the dining room. One table was lined with papers displayed in chronological order. The second table closest to the parlor stove held his new Remington typewriter and the large family Bible.

"Pardon my inquiry, but you are here every night into the wee hours of the morning. What are you working on?" The young headmaster, who led a sheltered life, was fascinated by this independent, world traveler, and free thinker.

"It is my opus magnus, the culmination of thirty years of research and interviews with Karl Marx."

"I have heard the name. Is he a utopian fighting for workers' rights in Europe?"

"I originally believed so. Yes, women and children work long hours in dangerous settings for starvation wages in factories and mills while the owners make fortunes."

"Like our illustrious Mr. Vanderbilt, Mr. Carnegie, and Mr. Rockefeller?" Mr. Bennett interjected.

"Exactly. Our nation was established as an agrarian society. Farmers work from sunrise to sunset. I have seen this with my own family. They create their own wealth; someone else is not getting rich from their labors.

Now we are experiencing waves of immigration from our farms into our cities, and from Europe to our American cities in search of employment in factories. Fryeburg and Concord are a far cry from New York City," Thaddeus continued.

"I agree. We work for ourselves or for our neighbors. But can we not make new laws to protect these workers from abuse?" Mr. Bennett questioned.

"Yes. I believe in reform – shorter hours, safer conditions, and higher pay. But Marx is not promoting reforms, he is inciting revolution. He intends to destroy the capitalist system, eliminate personal property."

"But how? My grandfather, father and uncle worked hard for decades to establish a successful publishing company, took financial risks, provided employment for others," Mr. Bennett defended his family's wealth.

"Marxists would have the government take their business," Thaddeus shook his head.

"But how?"

"By force, revolution, or bloodshed. First, I thought he was a prophet. I devoted years of my life reading his writings, listening to speakers, interviewing him. Slowly I realized that he is a madman. His ideas will only lead to bloodshed, misery, loss of property, dignity, freedom and perhaps millions of lives." Thaddeus stood up and began pacing.

"Then you must write a book denouncing him." Mr. Bennett walked over to the table of his notes. "Rather than write your ideas in chronological order, expose the dangers of his ideology, refute them, and propose your own constructive solutions."

Thaddeus looked at the young man with newfound respect.

"May I assist you with the proofreading and editing of your manuscript? I happen to know a publisher who might be interested," he grinned. Pointing to the family Bible, "I did not take you to be a religious man."

"I am not. However, my grandmother was a godly woman and an influence in my life."

"Do you mean the Senator's wife?"

"She was much more than a senator's wife. She was a Quaker, an abolitionist, an educator, a faithful wife and loving mother and grandmother. She lived her faith. I should have listened to her."

"If you feel so strongly, why do you not attend church?"

"Then I would have to admit that she was right, and I was wrong. I will go to church if you come with me," Thaddeus challenged.

"I go to church. I've attended both the Unitarian and the Swedenborg church."

"True. But Summer only attends the Congregational Church," he teased.

Emerson wondered what his friends and family back in Concord would say. "Only if we sit in the back row and leave before the ending of the last hymn."

---------❋---------

Thaddeus and Emerson sheepishly slipped into the last row of the Congregational Church. Mrs. Charles nudged her husband and whispered, "I never thought I'd see the day when Thaddeus Pierce would return to church."

Several Academy students smiled warmly at the headmaster as they walked past. Charlie, and Summer entered as the first bell struck.

"Mr. Bennett! Mr. Bennett! Come sit up front with us!" Charlie loudly and excitedly invited.

Reluctantly, the headmaster followed the siblings up the aisle.

"You can use my hymnal because I know all the songs by heart. Singing is good, very good."

Summer's smile made him forget his unease. Charlie grabbed his sleeve, "Mr. Bennett, Mr. Bennett, sit by me!"

Emerson found himself sitting between Charlie and Summer. Daniel and Emily joined them while Jeremy and his mother found seats next to Thaddeus.

"Make sure you listen! Uncle Danny always asks us questions about the sermon," Charlie warned.

To Emerson's dismay the good pastor preached a sixty-minute treatise on the doctrines delineated in the Nicene Creed. Being raised in the Unitarian Church, he rejected the doctrine of the Trinity. How can Jesus be fully God and fully man?

He sighed as Reverend Mason began to reiterate because of the Fall, all people are born sinners and need a Savior. Clearly, the pastor had never read *Origins of Species* by Charles Darwin. It was his duty to educate this naïve pastor.

He inwardly cringed as he listened to the story of the resurrection of Christ. Perhaps he was most distraught to hear the doctrine of the Second Coming, and the resurrection of the dead. How can educated, modern people believe such superstitions? It was his responsibility to enlighten his students to modern thought and help them reject these fallacies! He was most grateful to sing the last hymn and leave!

During Sunday dinner Thaddeus asked, "So Emerson, what did you think of the sermon?"

He glanced at Daniel and Emily, who he loved and respected, Mrs. Chase, the best cook in the world, and Jeremy, who was like a younger brother. He chose his words carefully.

"Frankly, I found it rather disconcerting. As you know I was raised in the Unitarian Church and my father was heavily involved in the Transcendental Movement back in Concord. It contradicted most everything I was taught."

"It confirmed everything I was taught," Thaddeus stated. Emerson was uncertain if he was sincere or simply starting controversy. "Have you ever read the Bible? You cannot reject something you never read."

"Well said. I tell my students that all the time," Emerson agreed.

What did he get himself into?

Emerson decided to pay a visit to Reverend Mason on his way home from school Monday afternoon.

"Mr. Bennett! What a welcomed surprise. To what do I owe this honor?" the kind pastor greeted as he motioned to take a seat.

"I brought a book for you to read. I thought you may find this to be enlightening." He handed the pastor *Origin of Species* by Charles Darwin.

"Thank you. What did you think of the sermon?"

"Well, I was raised in the Unitarian Church which rejects the idea of the Trinity. Are you not worshipping three gods?"

"I understand that your denomination rejects the Trinity. But what does the Bible say?"

"I do not know, for I never read the Bible," Emerson admitted.

"May I suggest that you read the first chapter of the Gospel of John? I will read your book and we will have tea and a discussion next Monday," Reverend Mason invited.

On his walk home, he met Summer who was exiting the General Store. "Mr. Bennett, it was lovely to see you in church yesterday. Would you like to come to Sunday dinner next week. Charlie would be thrilled to have you visit."

"Miss Miller, I am looking forward to it."

That evening Emerson found Thaddeus writing letters – one in German, one in Hebrew and one in English. "Do you have pen pals?" he asked.

"I have two sons and a grandson. Josef lives in Austria," he held up the letter in German. "Natan lives in Warsaw. I know neither Polish nor Yiddish, so we correspond in Hebrew. My grandson, Joshua who also lives in Poland, is learning English." He noticed the perplexed expression on Emerson's face. "It is a long story which I will tell you another day. Have you come to discuss Marxism?"

"Mr. Miller says you have borrowed the family's Bible. If you are not reading, may I?"

"The whole Bible?"

"Of course not. Just the Gospel of John." Emerson tentatively turned the pages of the tome.

"John is in the New Testament. Matthew, Mark, Luke, and John." Thaddeus explained as he quickly opened to John 1:1. "My grandmother taught me," he explained sheepishly and turned to letter writing.

In the beginning was the Word, and the Word was with God, and the Word was God.

The same was in the beginning with God.

All things were made by him; and without him was not anything made that was made.

In him was life; and the life was the light of men.

And the light shineth in darkness; and the darkness comprehended it not.

There was a man sent from God, whose name was John.

The same came for a witness, to bear witness of the Light, that all men through him might believe.

He was not that Light, but was sent to bear witness of that Light.

That was the true Light, which lighteth every man that cometh into the world.

He was in the world, and the world was made by him, and the world knew him not.

He came unto his own, and his own received him not.

But as many as received him, to them gave power to become the sons of God, even to them that believe on his name:

Which were born, not of blood, nor of the will of the flesh, nor of the will of man, but of God.

And the Word was made flesh, and dwelt among us, (and we beheld his glory, the glory as of the only begotten of the Father,) full of grace and truth

"Was John a rabbi?" Emerson asked.

"No, he was a fisherman."

How could a fisherman write so elegantly? It was like the finest poetry he ever read. Emerson read the entire Gospel of John before going to bed.

The next evening, he stopped in the dining room to talk with Thaddeus.

"What book in the Bible are you reading tonight?" Thaddeus teased.

"None. I came to see how you are doing with your manuscript." Emerson took a seat in a nearby dining room chair.

"I have so much material, I am overwhelmed."

"Marx had ten ideas. Begin with the easiest to refute," Emerson suggested.

"That would be # 3 *Abolition of all rights to inheritance*. The man refused to work to support his wife and children. He demanded money from his upper middle-class parents and financial support from his partner, Fredrich Engels. But he refused to work. His wife and children suffered from the lack of money, lack of food, a lack of a steady roof over their heads, and lack of medical attention. I remember when their one-year-old son died. I dare say it was from neglect. I heard his wife once say, 'Karl, if you had only spent more time making capital instead of writing about it, we would be better off.'[1.]

His mother outlived his father by twenty years. Marx hired a lawyer to secure his future inheritance. Upon his mother's death, he received $6000 in gold and German francs."[2.]

"So, the man who refused to work, demanded that other people work to support him?" Emerson asked in disbelief.

"Apparently it takes capitalism to finance socialism."

"The man who wants to abolish inheritance, hired an attorney to secure his inheritance! I think that might be a good place to start," Emerson suggested.

---❋---

Seeking

Charlie was waiting for Mr. Bennett on the granite steps of the Congregational Church the next Sunday morning. "Mr. Bennett, Mr. Bennett, I waited for you!"

"I see that," he smiled.

"Cousin Thaddeus, Papa says you are family, and you should sit in the family pew. Uncle Danny is saving you a seat."

As Thaddeus and Emerson took their seats, Mrs. Walker poked her husband, "I do not believe my eyes. Not only did Thaddeus Pierce return to church, but he is also sitting in the family pew!" she whispered.

Charlie placed himself between Cousin Thaddeus and Mr. Bennett. "You can use my hymnal, Cousin, because I know all the words. Summer and Mr. Bennett will share a hymnal."

It was difficult for Mr. Bennett to admit that he did enjoy the singing. Sharing a hymnal with Summer made it just more enjoyable.

"The text for today's sermon is taken from the first chapter of the Gospel of John. *In the beginning was the Word, and the Word was with God, and the Word was God.*

The same was in the beginning with God.

All things were made by him; and without him was not any thing made that was made.

In him was life; and the life was the light of men.

And the light shineth in darkness; and the darkness comprehended it not.

Who or what is the Word?"

"I was thinking that to myself." Charlie whispered a little too loudly.

The Pastor looked down from his pulpit. "It is a wonderful thing to ask questions, Charlie. That is how we learn. More people should ask questions."

"So, what is the Word?" Charlie asked.

"Jesus Christ is the Word. Let us read the passage aloud and substitute 'Jesus' for the 'Word and him.'"

In unison the congregation read *"In the beginning was Jesus, and Jesus was with God, and Jesus was God.*

The same was in the beginning with God.

All things were made by Jesus; and without Jesus was not anything made that was made.

In Jesus was life; and the life was the light of men.

And the light shineth in darkness; and the darkness comprehended it not"

"That is good, very, very good," Charlie approved.

It did not matter that Sunday dinner was rather bland, for Emerson was there for the company, and not the food.

"Mahayla, how is the apothecary business coming along?" Emerson asked for he observed her and Jeremy spending most evenings in Emily's kitchen, measuring and labeling herbs, concocting salves, and tinctures.

Her face brightened. "Jeremy is a wonderful salesman. We have accounts in stores in Portland, Saco, Biddeford, and Bridgton, plus several doctors along the route have purchased salves and tinctures. He leaves tomorrow for Conway, Tamworth, Ossipee and Wolfeboro in New Hampshire. Some of our bigger customers telegraph their reorders. Summer is helping me keep the books."

Emerson turned to Summer, "You are certainly one busy lady! Between running your father's office and assisting your sister, how do you have time to work on your writing?"

Seeking

"Mr. Bennett, what is that book?" Charlie interrupted.

"It is *The Adventures of Tom Sawyer* by Mark Twain. It is about a mischievous boy who is always in trouble. I brought it for you to read."

Charlie flipped through the pages. "Reading is hard, very hard," he said sadly.

"I think you and an adult can read it aloud together. There are some words you can read." He opened to the first chapter and handed the book to him.

"*Tom!*" Charlie began.

"*No...*

"The word is answer," Mr. Bennett sounded it out for him.

"*No answer.*

"*Tom!*"

No answer." Charlie read triumphantly.

"*What's gone with that boy, I wonder? You Tom!*"

No answer."

Charlie looked up from the book and grinned, "I am reading!"

———— ✽ ————

Monday afternoon Emerson knocked on Reverend Mason's office door.

"Come in. Come in. The teapot is ready as I promised," he greeted. "I am eager to hear your response to yesterday's sermon," he poured a cup of tea for his guest.

"You have convinced me that the Bible clearly states that Jesus and God are one. However, I don't believe the Bible."

"Interesting. This will be our little secret. We would not wish for the Trustees of the Academy to learn of this. What do you believe, Mr. Bennett?"

Although Emerson was quite certain in what he disbelieved, he had no idea in what he did believe.

"Um…My father was active in the Transcendental Movement when he was a young man. Ralph Waldo Emerson, Henry David Thoreau, Bronson Alcott, Nathaniel Hawthorne all highly regarded authors broke off from Unitarianism."

"I can understand how a young publisher could be swayed by famous authors. That is who you believe in, but not the beliefs themselves. What did they and you believe?"

"Decades ago, they formed a commune, a farm named Brook Farm in West Roxbury where everyone equally shared in the work and the produce."

"I'm sure Eli Miller would be interested in visiting such a place. Perhaps you could take him for a visit."

"Well, the farm only lasted for a few years," Emerson confessed.

"That is what they did. What did they believe?"

"First, everyone is born essentially good. We don't believe we are born sinners. We all have some divinity in us."

"Is that not what Universalists believe that everyone is going to heaven? If you reject the doctrine of original sin, then you reject our need for a Savior to save us from our sins."

"Exactly," Emerson was relieved to finally express his ideology. "Also, truth can be experienced through personal experience and not found in one book written thousands of years ago."[3.]

"Do you believe that truth varies from one person's experience to another's? Can truth vary and still be true? If your truth is the Bible is a fallible, old document written by fallible men and my truth is the Bible is the infallible Word of God, can both of us be right? Can two conflicting views both be true? If some people believe that slavery is good – that is their truth and we believe that slavery is evil – that is our truth, then can both truths be true?" Reverend Mason challenged.

Emerson frowned for he did not know how to respond.

"Genesis Chapters one and two describes nature and humanity as creations of God, not as divine themselves, contradicting the ideas of the divinity of nature and humanity. The Bible also does not teach that the Christians should discover truth based on his or her intuition or imagination. In fact, Proverbs 3:5 famously admonishes believers to 'lean not on your own understanding.' As it says in Jeremiah 17:9, 'The heart is deceitful above all things.' Romans 3:10-12 clearly states that humans are in a deprived state. Romans 8:22 explains even nature suffers under the effects of sin. This goes against the transcendentalist idea of intrinsic goodness.

Rebellion against God is as old as the Garden of Eden. You may call it truth. The Bible calls it sin. Now take Charles Darwin and *The Origin of Species*."

Emerson brightened. "Did you have the opportunity to read it?"

"Yes, but nowhere did he define the term species. Does he mean kind as in Genesis where the Bible says God made everything according to its own kind? I don't believe that one kind of animal can turn into another kind of animal. Go visit Eli Miller, and he will explain how the Millers bred the largest and strongest horses over the decades. But never did he turn a horse into a goat or a chicken.

Darwin calls it 'natural selection'.[4.] Can nature create nature? Where is the supernatural? Where is the Creator? I fear since Mr. Darwin rejects the God of the Bible, he must create an alternative explanation for creation.

I am sorry if this disappoints you. Perhaps you may ask Dr. Miller to read it. As a man of science, he may have different insights. This week I would like you to read the first two chapters of the Gospel of Luke."

On his walk home Emerson spied Dr. Miller's carriage in the stable and entered the waiting room.

Lydia greeted him, "Mr. Bennett, are you ill? Do you need to see the doctor?"

"I am fine, thank you. I would like to drop off a book for Dr. Miller to read." He was disappointed that Summer was not there.

That evening Emerson found Thaddeus typing his manuscript. "Would you care to read my chapter on inheritance? It is only a rough draft.

"I would be honored. What are you working on now?"

"I am completing a chapter on Marx's tenth proposal of *free education for all children in public schools. Abolition of children's factory labor in its present form*."

"I think both of us agree with that," Emerson pointed out.

"Exactly. I wrote that public schools were first established in Massachusetts Colony in 1647 where there were fifty or more households. In towns of one hundred households, they were to support grammar schools of higher education.[5] My grandfather was the first headmaster of Fryeburg Academy back in 1792. The goal of education was to produce a literate society who could read the Bible for themselves, and not depend on priests or ministers to read and interpret the Bible for them."

Seeking

"Also, a literate society was essential to the American Revolution. Those who control education will control society a generation later." Emerson added.

"Emerson, you are brilliant! If the followers of Karl Marx establish and control the schools, then they will raise a generation of followers of Marx. After a few generations, society will become Biblically illiterate and naively accepting of socialism."

"Thaddeus, are you sure you are not a religious man?"

"I know my Bible very well; I simply choose to live life my own way. Whereas you have not read the Bible and you are uncertain what to believe."

"That reminds me. I have been assigned to read the first two chapters of the Gospel of Luke. Was Luke a Jewish fisherman like John?"

"No, he was a Gentile doctor," Thaddeus shook his head. "Pardon me for saying this, but how can such an educated man be so uninformed?"

"That is a profound question. I shall purchase my own Bible to study. I cannot reject what I have not learned. I will earn the right to reject it. Luke is the book before John, right?"

As Emerson surmised, this Sunday's sermon was taken from the first two chapters of the Gospel of Luke. However, he was thinking about his Sunday dinner with Dr. Miller and family.

---❋---

Over a meal of boiled ham, potatoes and carrots, Charlie began the conversation. "Why did Reverend Mason tell the Christmas story? It is not Christmas time."

Emerson took the opportunity to display his newfound knowledge. "Last week's sermon from John was to illustrate that Jesus Christ was God…"

"Everybody knows that! We're not stupid!"

"Do not interrupt, Charlie," Isaac reprimanded.

"This week's lesson was to illustrate the humanity of Christ through the story of the angel appearing to the young virgin, the immaculate conception, his birth in Bethlehem," Emerson explained.

"Charlie, after dinner please help your sisters with the dishes while Mr. Bennett and I take our tea in my office."

"I'm not stupid. I can do the dishes all by myself."

They took their seats in Isaac's inner office. The doctor initiated the conversion. "I am a doctor and a man of science," he nodded to the bookcase containing his medical books, the table with his microscope, and the shelves holding jugs of various medicines. "This book you lent me is no science book."

"Sir?"

"Louis Pasteur is a scientist."

"Who?"

"Louis Pasteur is a French scientist who discovered microbes that were causing wine and milk to spoil. Through a series of experiments, he was able to kill these germs which we call bacteria, by heating the liquid. This prevented the spoilage. It took many experiments, observations, and recording the data before he discovered the correct temperature.

A few years ago, he invented a vaccine for chicken cholera. Most recently he successfully vaccinated a young boy from rabies who was bitten by a rabid dog."[6.]

"That is amazing."

Isaac continued, "Joseph Lister is a British surgeon who read Pasteur's publications on germ theory. Surgery was only performed as last resort because so many patients died of infections. To combat infections, he began to employ cleanliness techniques used by Florence Nightingale."

"The famous nurse?"

"Yes. He kept the surgical environment clean, changed dressing and washed his hands. After reading the works of Pasteur he made the connection between germs and surgical wounds.

Fifteen years ago, he began using carbolic acid to treat compound fracture wound, for hand washing, treatment of surgical acid and even the air in the operating room. These measures drastically cut down the instances of infections and deaths.[7.]

Look at this," Isaac placed a glass slide in his microscope.

Mr. Bennett tentatively peered through the instrument. "What am I looking at?"

"Tetanus bacteria from Mr. Chase's wound. This is what killed him."

The young headmaster jumped back in terror.

"Just as Pasteur invented a vaccine for rabies, I am researching a vaccine for tetanus. I fear a simple country doctor, like me, does not have the time, talent, or resources to do so.

This is science. Your Mr. Darwin is no scientist!" he returned to his desk and held up the book. "This is a philosophy book, not a science book! Where are the observations? The data? The experiments? None of this can be proven."

"Can you disprove it?" Emerson challenged.

"Yes. Blood clotting," Isaac responded.

"I do not understand, sir."

"There are some processes so complicated in the human body, it must work exactly right the very first time. You cannot make the process any simpler. We are only now beginning to understand the complexities of blood clotting.

What would happen if you cut your finger?"

"It would bleed, of course," Emerson answered.

"How would you treat it?"

"I would get a clean rag, apply pressure and it would stop bleeding."

"That is because our Creator created our blood with the ability to clot on its own. What would happen if your blood could not clot?

"You would bleed to death?" Emerson had never thought about this before.

"Precisely. There is a rare blood clotting disorder called hemophilia where the blood does not have the ability to clot properly. A minor accident could leave the patient bleeding to death.

Blood must have the ability to circulate throughout the body. On the other extreme, if the blood forms huge clots for no reason, preventing the blood from circulating properly, the patient can die. Blood clotting must perfectly work the first and every time.

What is Mr. Darwin's explanation? How did natural selection create this? Doctors are only beginning to learn about blood clotting. Only an omniscient Creator could create such a complex process. Now take the human eye…"

"I see your point, sir. Fryeburg is indeed fortunate to have such a learned doctor."

Seeking

The dejected young man was not looking forward to his Monday afternoon appointment with minister.

"Perfect timing. The tea is ready. Mr. Bennett, I confess that I do look forward to our chats," he invited his visitor.

"Sir, you will be pleased to hear that our friend Charlie listened and understood your sermon."

"He is a remarkable boy in many ways. My question is, did you listen and understand it?"

"Your sermons are quite clear," Emerson complimented.

This week's assignment is to read the second chapter of Acts."

"Let me guess. The Holy Spirit?"

"See you next week," Reverend Mason smiled.

Daniel met Emerson as he arrived home in time for supper and asked, "I was at the post office this morning and I took the liberty of bringing this package home for you. Is it another book?"

"It is my Bible. I cannot reject what I do not know. I must earn the right."

XXII

Commitments

It was the spring of 1881 when Emerson was surprised to find no tea waiting for him in Reverend Mason's office. "Excuse me, Reverend, is this not Monday afternoon?"

"Indeed, it is, and it is time for you to decide. After a year of inquiry and faithful church attendance, you need to decide if you will officially become a church member."

"But why? You said I am a faithful attendee. What is the difference?"

"Commitment. It is the difference between being an admirer and being a husband."

Emerson blushed.

"What are the reasons for your indecisions? Are you afraid your friends and family back in Concord will not approve? Who do you wish to honor? The Lord or Ralph Waldo Emerson?

Are you being fair to Miss Miller? Half the eligible bachelors in Fryeburg would be honored to take her hand in marriage. Yet you monopolize her time and attentions preventing her from socializing with other fine young men.

You are an outstanding preceptor at the Academy and are held in esteem by the community. A man cannot live by books alone. The difference between a man and a boy is commitment. Good day, sir," the pastor dismissed him.

The dejected young man slowly walked towards home.

"Mr. Bennett! Mr. Bennett! Why are you so sad?" Charlie ran from his backyard followed by Charlie Dog. "When I was sad, Grandpa and I would sit and talk. Let's sit on the bench under the elm tree."

How Emerson grew to love this boy during the past six years! He took a seat and asked, "Charlie why do you love Easter?"

"Because even though we are sinners and do wrong things, God still loves us. He decided to send His son to be born. That is Christmas."

"I know that" he smiled.

"Everybody knows that. But that is not the end of the story. Everybody gets born and we are not Jesus."

"Sir, that is a profound observation."

"He told everybody about God. Some people believed and followed. Some people made fun of Him. When people make fun of me and call me an idiot I think about Jesus. He would never hit a boy over the head with his slate."

"Another profound observation."

"Do you know that in the olden days Jewish people would kill lambs to say sorry to God? But they had to keep killing those poor sheep because they always were sinners. Uncle Danny says Jewish people don't kill lambs anymore, unless they eat them for supper. It is like Uncle Eli hunting for deer so the family can eat supper.

I like venison but I don't think I would like hunting. Do you?"

"I have never gone hunting. I do not think that I would like it either," Emerson agreed.

"Jesus is called the Lamb of God. When he died on the cross for our sins, Jewish people could stop killing sheep – unless it was for supper. Nana and Grandpa died. Everybody dies. But we're not Jesus."

"You are an insightful young man."

"That is not the end of the story. On the third day, He rose from the dead. He was not just a nice man, a very, very nice man. He was God. Lots of people saw him and talked to him. Then one day He went back to heaven.

I forgot. Before he went back to heaven, He said that in His Father's House there are many rooms. Uncle Danny says that means Heaven. When He went back to Heaven, He saved a room for us. Uncle Danny says it is like making a reservation at the Oxford House. The room is ready for people who believe in Easter. When I get to Heaven, Jesus will say, 'Charlie, your room is ready.' I hope my room is next to Grandpa's."

"Charlie, my friend, I feel much better." Emerson stood up.

"Where are you going?"

"To tell Reverend Mason that I believe in Easter, and I will join the church."

"I will go with you!"

Summer heard the entire conversation through her open bedroom window.

———❋———

That evening Emerson knocked on Isaac's office door. "What a welcomed surprise. I am afraid that Summer is not here. She, Mahayla, and Mrs. Miller went to a Women's Temperance

Meeting with my sister. Charlie is upstairs getting into mischief I imagine. He and I have an understanding; if he is quiet and I can get some work done, I can overlook any boyish misbehavior," he chuckled.

"Sir, I did not come to see Summer. I came to speak to you. As you know, I have grown very fond of Summer recently. I dare say she is rather fond of me. I would like to ask you for her hand in marriage."

"I have two responses. First, what took you so long?" he laughed. "Secondly, you have my blessing."

The door flung open. "This is the happiest day of my life! I always wanted a big brother! Let's go ask Summer right now!"

"Benjamin Charles Miller! How many times have I told you not to listen to adults' conversations! It is Emerson's job to propose marriage, not yours."

Charlie ignored the reprimand. "This is what we need to do. Plan a picnic. Girls like picnics. Everybody knows that."

"Not all girls," Emerson contradicted as he pictured Lily with her hoop skirts, bustle, and white gloves.

"And we will pick her some flowers. The forsythia is in bloom. Do you have a ring? We need a ring."

"I have my grandmother's ring." He failed to mention that his mother had given it to him with the intent of giving it to Lily.

"We can ask her tomorrow after school."

"No. Emerson will ask her tomorrow, not you," Isaac contradicted.

Charlie started to pout. "Would you like to go with Emerson and spend the night with Uncle Danny and Aunt Emily?" With Charlie out of the house, he could not reveal the secret in advance.

"I think that is a wonderful idea!" Emerson agreed. "We can put a mattress on the floor in my room. Charlie Doll and Charlie Dog can come too."

Emerson thought the school day would never end! Charlie had the event planned: he picked a bouquet of forsythia while Mrs. Chase packed a picnic lunch and Emerson had the ring carefully wrapped in a linen handkerchief in his pocket. It was a glorious, spring afternoon as he walked down the granite steps of Fryeburg Academy.

His heart was pounding as he knocked on the kitchen door and Summer answered. "Emerson, thank you for your note last night. I think a picnic is a lovely idea. There is a nice shady spot by the Saco at the farm where we always had picnics as children," she smiled as she grabbed an old quilt with one hand and took his arm with the other."

Emerson was relieved that Charlie was nowhere to be found, when they picked up the picnic basket from Mrs. Chase and continued down the road to the farm. Summer laid the quilt down on the grass beside some bushes. She gracefully sat by his side. Even wearing a simple, cotton dress she was beautiful. The two of them silently ate their food while gazing at the river.

Suddenly, the bushes stirred, and Charlie yelled, "What are you waiting for? Ask her!"

Emerson blushed. He took the ring from his pocket and asked, "Summer Miller will you do me the honor and become my wife?"

Jeremy and Mahayla poked their heads around the bushes. "You should marry him." Mahayla urged.

Commitments

"He is not half as pompous as he used to be. You could do worse!" Jeremy laughed.

"Hurry up. Uncle Eli and Aunt Julia are having a big party. Everybody is waiting for you!" Charlie led the way.

Emerson had not noticed all the wagons and carriages parked in the dooryard. "How…"

Mahayla explained, "Charlie went to the general store this morning to tell Aunt Rachel. The ladies Missionary Society overheard the conversation and spent all morning spreading the good news. Half of Fryeburg has heard already. Reverend Mason says September is a wonder time for a wedding!"

---❋---

Thaddeus entered the front parlor. "Danny, remember when I asked you if I could stay a few months?"

"I believe it was five years ago."

"The book is finished. Bennett Publishing has estimated it will be out next spring."

"Congratulations. That is quite an accomplishment. Frankly, I did not think you could do it."

"Why not?" he responded defensively.

"I knew you were capable. However, you spent your life traveling from place to place, from one assignment to another. I have never seen you stay in one place, working for so long, committed to one project."

"If that surprised you, then you will be more surprised to learn I was offered an editing job at the New York Post to begin in February. No more traveling the world for me. I will spend my remaining days settled in one place, sitting at a desk. There is a large Jewish population in New York City. I hope if my children move to America, they will feel at home."

"It will feel strange to have both you and Emerson gone."

"You still have Jeremy."

"I am thankful for that. I hope your children visit soon."

"So do I!"

❋

"Mr. Miller, there is a matter which I wish to discuss with you," Jeremy approached Daniel.

"Let us talk in the parlor. I also have a matter to discuss."

"After Emerson moves into the Headmaster's House, would it be possible for me to move up into his living quarters? I intend to ask Mahayla to marry me. My mother says there should only be one bride at a time in the family. She suggested that I wait until Christmas to propose. I cannot afford to buy a house right now. If we could live here, we can continue to use the kitchen for our products, store the peddler wagon in the stable, and walk to the herb garden."

"Emily and I do not know what we would have done without you and your mother. It is much more than cooking, cleaning, and chores; you are family. We have grown to love you as a grandson.

Tomorrow Mrs. Miller and I will make an appointment with Attorney Hastings to update our will. You will inherit this house with some stipulations. First, your mother continues to live here.

I do not imagine that Charlie will be able to live alone. Once my brother is gone, I want you to take Charlie in and be responsible for him."

"Charlie is like the younger brother I never had. Of course, Mahayla and I will care for him. Mr. Miller."

"One more thing, my cousin Thaddeus will always be welcomed here and will have his own room available."

"Mr. Miller, I do not know what to say!"

"Jeremy, your actions speak for themselves."

If anyone thought three months was not sufficient time to plan a proper wedding, they did not know the Miller ladies!

The vacant Headmaster's home was scrubbed clean from top to bottom. Julia gave the couple the Liberty Table, claiming it took up too much space in the kitchen, and Aunt Grace's one-hundred-year-old dining room set, declaring it was too old-fashioned. She had her own furniture in storage which she wanted to use.

Rachel had Summer select any fabric she wished to make curtains, and gave them a new icebox, slightly marred during shipping.

Emily devoted every waking moment measuring windows and sewing curtains on her Singer sewing machine.

Lydia retrieved the crates of white china rimmed with gold, which had belonged to Summer's great grandmother, Hannah Miller. She took down the four oil paintings which hung in her foyer, suggesting they would impress visiting guests. Summer remembered they were commissioned by her great grandfather, Senator Benjamin Miller, and painted by her grandfather's cousin, Sadie Miller.

Rachel organized a moving day, recruiting Jonathan, his two oldest sons, Jeremy, and Charlie and commandeered Eli's wagon.

Summer insisted on wearing her graduation dress on her wedding day. Emily made a new dress for Mahayla and the mother of the bride. Lydia took Charlie to the tailor for a brand-new suit. At Lydia's request, he also made a suit for Charlie Doll at no charge.

After Mrs. Bennett recovered from her initial dismay, she shipped her late husband's mahogany desk and crates of his books.

Jonathan and Jeremy built two large pine bookcases and delivered them to Emerson's new home office.

Numerous relatives from the Frye, Wiley, Evans, and Walker clans held a kitchen party where pots and pans, silverware, stoneware bowls, jugs, aprons, the latest kitchen gadgets, and cases of canned goods were cheerfully given.

A cake and lemonade reception was planned at the Academy for the students and community. The ladies of both the Congregational and New Church volunteered to make and serve the refreshments.

Mortified to learn of this "common" event for such a "distinguished" family, Mrs. Bennett made reservations for a proper high tea for family members only at the Oxford House, when she reserved rooms for her daughters and their families, her brother-in-law and his wife, and herself. She also arranged for respectable transportation from the train depot to the hotel!

Unbeknownst to Isaac, Lydia wisely asked Dr. Towle to handle any medical emergencies for that weekend. Yes, the Miller ladies were ready!

XXIII

A Wedding and a Tragedy

It was five minutes to one o'clock, and the horse and carriage were ready by the front door. The family gathered in the foyer as Summer descended the front staircase.

Isaac swallowed hard. When did his precious little girl mature into a beautiful woman?

"You look absolutely radiant," Lydia complimented.

"I hope Emerson realizes how lucky he is!" Mahayla declared.

Summer turned to her fifteen-year-old brother, "Charlie, look how handsome you are in your new suit!" He stood up straight.

'Well, it is time to go. Is everyone ready?"

"Isaac! Thank God, I caught you. Grab your bags and come with me! A pot of boiling water fell on my neighbor's toddler! I have never seen anything like this – not even in the war.!" Ivory Snow, a Fryeburg farmer, and a war veteran was hysterical.

"Isaac, No! Not on your daughter's wedding day!" Lydia interrupted. "Doctor Towle is handling all emergencies this weekend. Call on his office!"

"I did, Mrs. Miller. He is treating a gunshot wound in East Fryeburg."

"What about Dr. Lamson? Try him," Lydia persisted.

"I did, after I learned Dr. Towle was unavailable. He is in Portland."

"No Isaac! I forbid it!"

"Papa, I understand. You need to go. Mama, how would you feel if I was that toddler and the only available doctor refused to come?"

"Who will walk you down the aisle?" Lydia demanded.

"I will," Charlie volunteered. "I am handsome, very handsome."

"I am not sure if – "

"I walk down that aisle every Sunday morning. I'm not stupid. I can walk down the aisle."

Summer slipped her arm through his. "I would be very proud to have you walk me down the aisle. Papa, you need to go."

He ran into his office and grabbed his two medical bags. "Ivory, I need you to take me in your wagon." He kissed his daughter on her cheek. "You are beautiful, simply beautiful."

It was fifteen minutes past one, and Emerson stood nervously in his new suit in front of the crowded church. His best man, Jeremy, stood beside him. "Do not worry. She will be here. Charlie is probably looking for Charlie Doll," he whispered.

The congregation looked at one another in awkward silence. Mrs. Bennett fumed. How dare this small-town girl humiliate her in front of the family! Her daughters whispered to one another.

Daniel quietly slipped out the door and headed down the steps, just as the carriage arrived. When he realized that Isaac was not there, he wisely said nothing. "Summer, you are beautiful." He assisted the ladies down from the carriage.

"I am walking Summer down the aisle. She says I am handsome." It was then he realized that he left Charlie Doll at home. "I have to be brave, very brave," he told himself. "I have to be brave for Summer."

"Lydia, may I have the honor of escorting you to your seat?"

Silently seething, she took her brother-in-law's arm.

The entire church turned around at the sound of the front door opening. After the mother of the bride was seated, the organ began, the congregation stood as Mahayla, the maid of honor, began her walk down the aisle followed by Summer and Charlie.

Mrs. Weston turned to her husband and whispered, "Can you imagine missing your daughter's wedding?" Murmurs spread throughout the church.

However, Emerson did not notice. He only had eyes for Summer.

———— ❋ ————

Ivory led Isaac to the back door of the Anderson's small farmhouse. The distraught father was pacing outside while yelling, "How could she let this happen? Why wasn't she watching him?"

Ivory quickly opened the kitchen door. The house was eerily silent; a large copper pot laid on its side on the floor in a puddle by the cookstove. A dozen mason jars were neatly lined up on the table. They walked through the deserted kitchen into the small parlor and found Mrs. Anderson in a rocking chair silently clutching the shaking toddler.

Isaac walked over and sat on a nearby chair. "I am Dr. Miller, and I am here to help your child. I need to exam him." There was no response. He carefully removed his jacket and vest and draped it over the chair. "I will not take him away. I need to treat him and then I will give him back," he explained kindly as he gently took the child out of the mother's arms.

He surmised the child was looking up at the pot when it overturned. The young face was badly burned by the scalding water; his eyes were blistered and blindly staring into space. His opened mouth was silently screaming, for his vocal cords had been burned. After gingerly placing him on the settee, he opened his doctor's bag. Isaac took the syringe and measured a small amount of opium.

Ivory wordlessly looked on in horror, as Isaac explained, "I need to apply some salve and bandages. Please go get Reverend Stone." Ivory ran out the front door, detached the wagon from the horse, and galloped back to the village.

Isaac took a tin of salve, made by Jeremy and Mahayla, with olive oil, dried comfrey leaves, calendula flowers, St. John's wort flowers and beeswax. Slowly and meticulously, he washed small sections of the burns on the child's face, neck, upper arms, and torso, and applied the salve. He was so focused he did not hear Ivory return with Reverend Stone.

A frightened little face peered through a bedroom door. "Hello, I am Reverend Stone, and I came to help your family. What is your name?"

"Etta."

"Etta, may I talk with you?"

As the ten-year-old- opened the door, three little faces appeared from behind the bed. "Did you see what happened." The four children shook their heads as they looked down at the floor. "Why don't we go to the backyard and let the doctor take care of your brother."

A Wedding and a Tragedy

There were over a hundred people enjoying lemonade and cake on the front lawn of the Academy. Alonzo Lewis, vice-president of the Board of Trustees, assumed the role of host of the event. He was sure to introduce the Bennett family to the other trustees, faculty, successful businessmen, and town leaders.

He walked over to Charlie who was standing by himself behind a tree. "I am not stupid. I am handsome, very handsome," he muttered.

"Charlie, come visit with the guests," Mr. Lewis invited.

He shook his head. "I am hiding from the mean ladies with the fancy dresses."

Emerson's aunt and uncle walked over.

"This must be Summer's brother," Mr. Robert Bennett shook Charlie's hand.

"Mr. Bennett, let me introduce you to Benjamin Charles Miller," Mr. Lewis intervened.

"You must be named after your great grandfather, Senator Benjamin Miller. Do you intend to follow in his footsteps?"

"Charlie is an apprentice in an apothecary business and works parttime at Evans General Store," Mr. Lewis continued.

"That is most impressive," Mrs. Bennett complimented. "When do you have time to go to school?"

Emerson walked over, holding a cup of lemonade. "I see you met my favorite student. I have enjoyed serving as his private tutor for the past five years."

Charlie smiled, "Mr. Bennett, I mean Emerson, is a very good teacher."

"It is a pity that your father missed the ceremony. But Summer was fortunate to have you walk her down the aisle. I do hope to meet him at tea," Emerson's aunt smiled.

Charlie learned that not all ladies with fancy dresses are mean.

When Isaac completed bandaging his patient, he gently placed him in his mother's arms. Silently she stared out the window as she rocked her child.

An expensive-looking carriage pulled up to the front door, and Dr. William Towle stepped down, clutching a large black leather bag.

"Excuse me, mam. I will be right back," Isaac stood up, feeling relieved when the older and more experienced doctor arrived.

The fifty-two-year-old was born in Fryeburg to the highly esteemed Dr. Ira Towle. After graduating from Fryeburg Academy, he went west to California in the early fifties to mine for gold. Upon his return, he studied and practiced medicine with his father. He served as a surgeon in the 12th and 23rd Regiments of Maine during the war. Isaac heard stories how he treated numerous soldiers who were badly burned in a massive explosion.[1.]

"Dr. Towle, thank you for coming."

"What are we dealing with?"

"A young child, who cannot be over the age of two, was badly scalded from an overturned pot of boiling water."

"I see." He quickly ascended the front steps followed by Isaac. "Mam, I am back. This is Dr. Towle. He has much experience with burn victims, and he will be helping me."

"I will take it from here, Dr. Miller. Thank you. I believe you have a wedding to attend."

"The child will need another dosage of morphine soon," Isaac informed.

"Thank you. He is my patient now."

Isaac entered the reception at the Oxford House, just as the waiters were serving tea. Emerson rose from the table, walked across the room, and pronounced, "Dr. Miller, sir, it is indeed an honor to be your son-in-law!" He led Isaac to the empty seat beside Lydia and across from Emerson's aunt and uncle.

"It is a pleasure to meet you," Robert Bennett greeted.

"Your son, Charlie, is the most delightful young man," Mrs. Robert Bennett praised.

"Thank you," he smiled. "Charlie a delightful young man?" he wondered as he watched his son quietly talking with Jeremy and politely sipping tea. Charlie Doll was nowhere to be seen.

The reception was a success; even Emerson's mother could find no fault.

Before the newlyweds departed, Mahayla announced, "I have been accepted to Medical School in New York. I will be leaving in January."

XXIV

New York

"Mahayla, please go into your father's office, I wish to speak with you." It took every ounce of self-control for Lydia to subdue her anger.

"Mother, there is nothing to talk about. I have made my decision."

"Perhaps it would be wiser, if we have this discussion tomorrow," Isaac suggested diplomatically. "It's been quite an emotional day."

"We will have this discussion now!" Lydia snapped and left for the office. Once seated, she turned to her husband, "Did you know about this?"

"Six years ago, she mentioned she wanted to become a doctor," he stated, "but I did not think anything of it."

"Why, because I am not as smart as Summer?" Mahayla accused.

"Certainly not. You were not inclined to excel at school. I did not believe you would succeed in medical school."

"I know more about medicine; I am more mature and responsible than you were at my age!" she countered. "What does Canterbury Tales and other frivolous classes have to do with medicine? I excelled in Latin. I have spent my entire life preparing for this moment. I am an adult now. You cannot stop me!"

"That is all true," Isaac reluctantly agreed. "How will you pay for tuition? How will you support yourself?"

"I have saved my earnings. I intend to sell my herb garden to Jeremy and half my partnership in the business."

"What about Jeremy?" Lydia asked.

"Obviously, he cannot attend Women's Medical School, because it is only for women. Besides, he no longer wants to become a doctor. He wants to stay in Fryeburg forever and start his own business."

Lydia turned to Isaac, "Do something!" she demanded.

"Mahayla, everything you say is true. However, I ask that you not make your final decision until we both visit the school and infirmary."

She looked at her father skeptically. "When will that be?"

"A week from today. I will ask Dr. Towle first thing Monday morning to take my cases for the week."

Two packed suitcases were waiting by the front door. Isaac warned, "Now Charlie, you know Mahayla and I are leaving for New York City today. I do not want you to make a scene at the train station."

"I am not going to the train station with you. Saturday is busy, very busy at the store. Uncle Peter needs me to go to the train station with him later to pick up a delivery of sewing machines. Of course, Aunt Rachel will need me to open the crates and set up the display for her. I cannot be late for work.

Aunt Rachel says Mama should take me to the tailors for another suit. Not as fancy as my wedding suit. I should save that for church. I need a work suit. Aunt Rachel says I need to look like a businessman, and not a farm boy.

Jeremy says there is no use making a fuss that you are leaving. You are stubborn, very stubborn. Once you make up your mind, you will never change it."

"Oh, really? What else did Jeremy say?" Mahayla did not conceal her annoyance.

"He told me Mama treats me like a baby, so I act like a baby. He told me to act my age. He told me while Papa is away, I am the man of the house. I need to bring in the firewood every day and lock the doors every night.

Jeremy is like my big brother."

"I thought Emerson was your big brother," Mahayla countered.

"If I can have two sisters, I can have two brothers. Everybody knows that."

———✷———

As the train left Fryeburg Station, Mahayla asked her father, "What made you decide to become a doctor?"

Isaac thought for a moment. "The war. Those brave doctors treated their patients under extraordinary circumstances – on the battlefield with bullets flying, in makeshift surgical theaters in barns, classrooms and church sanctuaries. It takes more courage to save a life, than to take a life.

Why do you want to become a doctor?" he asked his daughter,

"Nana. She took care of everyone. She taught me about the different herbs, how to make remedies, how the body works, what can go wrong, how remedies can alleviate suffering. It is truly a science. If she had a proper education, she could have been an incredible doctor! Yet knowledge, without compassion, is only half the job. I think women will be more compassionate doctors. Present company excluded."

"Medicine can be gory," her warned.

"I have helped Uncle Eli and Jonathan gut their deer. They let me take the heart, brains, lungs, and intestines to dissect and study. One time I dissected an eye."

"When did you do all this?" he asked incredulously. "Why did I not know of this?"

"The past four hunting seasons. You were never around."

"That is my biggest regret becoming a doctor. I missed my children's childhoods. Summer is married, and you are off to New York.

How did you hear about this Dr. Blackwell?"

"Aunt Rachel," she smiled.

"Of course, it would be Rachel," he shook his head.

"Elizabeth Blackwell immigrated to America from England with her parents and siblings. They sound like an extraordinary family. She was the first woman in America to receive a medical degree. This was back in 1849, after she was turned down from every school she applied to, until she was accepted at Geneva College in upstate New York.[1] She never gave up.

Upon graduation, she could not find an internship anywhere in the country. She had to practice in Paris and then London,[2] before returning to New York City to open her own practice. Male doctors simply would not welcome her.

Meanwhile her younger sister, Emily also earned her medical degree and she had to move to Edinborough, Scotland for her internship. When she returned the two of them opened the New York Infirmary.[3]

Their goal was to provide medical care to poor families, and to provide internships to other women doctors. When they were not impressed with the caliber of education these women received, they decided to open Women's Medical School, College."[4]

"They sound like Aunt Rachel," Isaac mused.

"Aunt Rachel wants women to vote. Elizabeth Blackwell has other ideas. She believes, what good is a vote, if women do not know how to think independently? It is more important to prove the capacities of women and get them out of the shadow of menfolk."[5]

---❋---

Both Mahayla and Isaac were initially overwhelmed by the crowds, the variety of immigrants, the over-crowded and dirty tenements, the opulent homes of the wealthy, the tall buildings, the traffic, the noise, and smells of the city. However, they were both amazed by the New York Infirmary and the Women's Medical College.

A medical student gave them a tour of the new hospital, founded by the Blackwell sisters in 1857. The hospital moved to new quarters on Livingstone Place at the edge of Stuyvesant Square Park in 1876. This move allowed the school to expand into the newly vacated quarters.[6]

Isaac was envious of doctors working together, specializing in different areas with the newest medical and laboratory equipment. Imagine performing surgery in a sterile environment with other doctors or nurses by your side to assist! This made his medical practice in Fryeburg feel primitive and obsolete.

They were greeted at the Medical College by Dr. Mary Putnam Jacobi who gave them a brief history of the school. "It was never the intent of Dr. Elizabeth and Dr. Emily Blackwell to open a medical school. Because they needed to go to Europe for their residencies, they designed the Infirmary to treat patients, as well as serve as a residency for newly graduated female medical students. As you see it successfully serves this dual purpose."[7.]

There were already three women's medical colleges in existence, in Philadelphia, Boston, and here in New York. The Blackwells were disappointed with the poorly educated graduates who came to them. They felt they had no choice but to start their own medical school."[8.]

"How does this school differ from the others?" Isaac inquired.

"First, it is a three-year program rather than two. The lectures build progressively from year to year, rather than repeat the first year's course during the second year. We also have male faculty members here. Students are tested annually by a board of examiners. As you can see, we uphold the highest of standards."[9.]

Isaac had to agree his daughter would receive a superior education than he had. When father and daughter looked at one another, they knew Mahayla would be attending Women's Medical College in January!

---❋---

On the train ride home Isaac asked, "What do you think of New York?"

"I could have never imagined so many people living in one place! The poor seem much poorer than those in Fryeburg; the rich are much richer! Of course, everyone in Fryeburg speaks English. I think it will be a challenge treating patients who speak different languages. What did you think of the school?"

"I am thoroughly impressed."

"You mean you will let me go?"

"You have my blessing. Of course, you would go with or without my blessing," he shook his head.

"What about Mama?"

"You leave your mother to me."

XXV

Changes

Upon their return, Isaac learned the tragic news that the Anderson toddler had died. The New Church purchased a little coffin, and Ivory Snow arranged for the burial in the cemetery on Menotomy Road. There was no funeral; Reverend Stone said a few words and prayers at the burial.

Lydia explained, "Mrs. Anderson did not attend. In fact, she did not say a word or leave her rocking chair for a week. Mr. Anderson is simply beside himself! He brought his wife to the Poor Farm two days ago.

Poor little Etta! Ten years old and responsible for her younger siblings and running the house. Some of the ladies from church plan to visit each day to teach her to run a proper household, and care for the younger children. I will ask Summer to tutor her a few afternoons per week.

When Etta is older, and all the younger children are in school, Rachel will hire her to work in the store. A young woman needs to learn a trade. That was Charlie's idea."

"It certainly appears everyone will be so busy when Mahayla leaves for New York," Isaac responded nonchalantly.

"Isaac, the city is crime-ridden and filthy!" Lydia argued.

"The city is huge. Indeed, there are some parts that are crime-ridden and filthy," he conceded. "However, both the College and Infirmary are in safe neighborhoods. Don't forget Thaddeus will be moving to New York in February. She will have an older, male relative nearby if she should require assistance."

Lydia gave him a 'we are not finished discussing this look'.

That evening, Lydia continued their conversation with Isaac and Mahayla while Charlie sat at the top of the stairs listening. "Mahayla, be realistic. A woman studying medicine!"

"I have spent my entire life preparing for this moment. I am an adult now. You cannot stop me!"

"Lydia, that is all true," Isaac agreed "The medical school is a most impressive institution."

Lydia turned to Isaac, "Do something!" she demanded.

"Mahayla has made her decision. There is nothing I can do but give her my blessing."

"It certainly is different not having Emerson here," Thaddeus lamented. "I have grown rather fond of that young man." The family was seated in the front parlor.

"Fortunately, we still have Jeremy," Emily smiled at the despondent young man. "When do you plan to move to the third floor?"

"I am in no hurry."

"How about first thing Monday morning? Charlie would be excited to help," Daniel offered. "Perhaps we could build a pantry on the third floor to store your salves, teas and tonics and baskets of dried herbs."

"That's an excellent idea," Emily agreed enthusiastically, for this enterprise was over running her kitchen.

"I could build the shelves," Thaddeus offered.

"You?" everyone laughed.

"I am a man of many talents. Speaking of talents… What is this about Mahayla going to medical school and becoming a doctor?"

"I cannot imagine Lydia allowing her to go!" Emily declared.

"I see that I am not the only prodigal in the family," Thaddeus laughed. "I will be moving to New York as well. I will be available to visit and keep a watchful eye on her."

"I doubt that will make Lydia feel better," Mrs. Chase concluded.

"Jeremy, may I have a word with you," Daniel stood up and headed to the third floor.

"Mr. Miller, I no longer need to move up here. Feel free to rent it out to someone else," Jeremy stated glumly.

"Jeremy, perhaps you were wrong to postpone your marriage proposal. She may believe she has no future with you, and decided to make other plans with her life. You should march over there and tell her how you feel."

"Sir, you do not know Mahayla the way I do. Once she has made up her mind, there is no changing it. Even if I was able to, she would spend the rest of her life resenting me. She is not like Summer."

"No, she is like her Aunt Rachel," Daniel acknowledged. "Do you know my sister left the farm as a young woman to work in a textile mill in Biddeford? My mother was heartbroken, and beside herself with worry. I imagine Peter was also unhappy."

"What did Mr. Evans do?"

"Nothing. He let her go, and she returned home a few years later a more mature and confident woman. They have been partners in life and business ever since."

"Mahayla has been a part of my life for as long as I can remember. But I need to let her go and follow her dreams, and not mine."

———❋———

Sunday mornings had never been the same for Charlie since Mahayla began attending New Church, and now Summer married, and on her honeymoon. Nevertheless, he put on his new suit and went downstairs.

"Charlie, we are not going to church this morning. Your mother has a headache, and I think it is best if I stay home with her."

"I'm still going to church. I can walk down an aisle by myself. I'm not stupid."

"No Charlie, you are not stupid."

Charlie was invited to Sunday dinner at Aunt Rachel's. "Thank you for inviting me," Charlie politely stated as he took his seat. "There is no dinner at home. Mama has a headache," he rolled his eyes.

"I have an important matter to discuss with you," Peter began. "As you know you have worked here for six years without pay."

"That is because you were keeping me out of trouble."

Peter chuckled, "I am not sure how successful I was with that! However, I think it is time to pay you for your work. Now you are older, more responsible, and able to work without

Changes

constant supervision. I appreciate that you can load all those heavy crates."

"You are getting old. You need help," Charlie observed.

"You also take great care of the horses."

"You are a help to me in unloading the crates, setting up displays and carrying packages for the customers," Rachel continued.

"If I work for you, can I still work in Nana's garden? Jeremy and Mahayla need my help. In fact, Jeremy says next year I can go on business trips with him and care for the horses."

Peter and Rachel exchanged glances. "Charlie did you ever hear the story about when I left Fryeburg to work in Biddeford?"

"Grandpa told me. My father was just a little boy and he cried and missed you."

"Well, do you know that Mahayla will be leaving Fryeburg in a few months to go to school?"

"I know. I heard them talking last night in the office. I listened," he confessed. "I think that made Mama's headache worse."

"Well, what do you think about that?"

"I am not a little boy. I am not going to cry. I will be sad, very sad. But Summer will be sad, so I will have to visit her. Jeremy will be very sad. I will have to work extra hard in the garden. Was Nana mad when you left?"

"Indeed, she was."

"Did she get over it?"

"Of course, she did."

"I hope Mama gets over this. But I don't think she will."

───────❋───────

"Jeremy, Can we talk in the parlor?" Mahayla asked that afternoon. "I wish to speak to you about Charlie. I am concerned about him after I leave."

"I promised your uncle that I will take good care of him."

"Uncle Danny?"

"Yes, he is leaving me the house in his will, with the stipulation that my mother and Mr. Pierce can live here and I take care of Charlie after your parents are gone. He will always have a job, a home, and a friend. I assume since Fryeburg already has three doctors, you will not be returning."

She was stunned at the news. "Frankly, I have not thought about my future. I have also come to discuss business; I wish to sell you the herb garden. I will no longer need it, but I do need the money. You will need the garden to supply the raw materials."

"That sounds reasonable. Once we agree upon a price, I will give you a down payment and then make monthly payments."

She would have preferred a lump sum. "I am sure we can work something out. Also, I wish to sell you my half of the business."

"What?"

"Half those teas, tonics and salves belong to me. If you prefer, I can take them to New York to sell."

Jeremy was speechless. Could he borrow money from Mr. Pierce or from Mr. Miller? "Yes, of course. That is only fair. I need time to think about this."

"You have three months. I do not leave until the first of January."

Changes

Monday morning Jeremy, Mahayla, and Charlie were making salves to replenish the supply Isaac had used. No one mentioned the absence of Charlie Doll, as Charlie was carefully melting the beeswax. "Uncle Peter is going to pay me to work for him."

"Charlie, that is wonderful."

"I told him I will still work for Jeremy caring for the gardens and making medicine."

Mrs. Chase entered the kitchen, "Jeremy there is a woman here to speak to you."

A young, petite woman wearing a simple cotton dress entered. "Mr. Chase, Mrs. Evans suggested I speak with you. My name is Elizabeth Jackson. My father was a Jackson, but my mother is a Walker. She graduated from Fryeburg Academy the same year as Dr. Miller.

When my father died six months ago, my mother decided to return to Fryeburg where we have family. My grandfather was a Walker, and my grandmother is a Bradley."

"You must be related to half the town," Mahayla laughed. "I am Mahayla Miller, and this is my brother, Charlie."

"You are the niece leaving for medical school. Mrs. Evans told me about you and the business. Mr. Chase, I am inquiring about working with you. I handled all the bookkeeping at my father's business in Portland."

"Miss Jackson, I am afraid that I cannot afford to hire you," Jeremy apologized.

"I do not wish to work for you. I said to work with you. I understand that Miss Miller will be leaving town, and you may need a business partner. I wish to invest some of my inheritance in shares of this business. I believe women can be successful business owners. I confess I have never worked in a garden, nor know anything about medicines. However, I have a strong work ethic, can handle the finances, and make any remedies following your recipes while you are away on sales visits."

"Miss Jackson, I work in the garden. You won't have to do that."

"Charlie, my friends call me Elizabeth."

Charlie smiled at the thought of having a new friend.

"I thought I could work with Mahayla making remedies during the next few weeks. On a trial basis, of course. If I meet your standards, then we can discuss a partnership, Mr. Chase."

"My friends call me Jeremy. Elizabeth, you have a deal."

"This is good news, very good news." Charlie beamed.

Mahayla was uncertain about this future venture. On the one hand, she could sell her share of the business and receive payment right away. On the other hand, she did not realize how easily she could be replaced.

That evening Eli came to speak with Mahayla "River View Farm has been in the Miller family for five generations. I just heard that you are selling part of it to someone outside the family. You should have discussed it with me first!" he stated crossly.

"Nana gave those gardens to me. If I choose to sell them, that is my business, not yours. I no longer have use for them, and I need the money. I am certainly within my rights," she countered.

"I do not question the legality of the sale. I question your loyalty to the family."

"I am family. I will buy it," Charlie intervened.

That solution pleased everyone.

Within three weeks, Jeremy offered the partnership to Elizabeth, Mahayla received her payment, and was no longer a business owner. Eleanor Jackson became good friends with Mrs. Chase, and the two widows spent much together. Harriet recommended that Lydia hire Eleanor part time to work in the office to compensate for the loss of Summer's help.

The next morning, Charlie left to work in the store, Isaac was busy with patients, and Lydia was training Mrs. Jackson in running the office. For the first time in her life, Mahayla had nothing to do!

"You might want to visit your sister," Lydia suggested. "Once you leave…"

"Good idea," she tried to sound cheerful. She found Summer seated at her "new" dining room table at a typewriter, Emerson's uncle gave for a wedding gift. "What are you typing?"

"My new novel. I try to write every free minute when Emerson is gone. Speaking of gone… It will be so different when you leave. Can you picture yourself living in New York?"

"To be honest, I found it overwhelming at first. Now I realize this is a chance in a lifetime! I am benefiting from the struggles and determination of women a generation before me."

"Nana would be so proud! I know I am!" Summer enthused.

"If only Mother could be," Mahayla rolled her eyes.

"Give her time. You had years to think about this; she has had two weeks. Mother Bennett gave us a horse and carriage," she nodded toward the stable.

"I guess she doesn't want to be met at the train station by a wagon and farm boys."

"Mahayla, that was most unkind. The carriage is greatly appreciated. Charlie stops by every day to feed and groom Charlie Horse."

"Let me guess. Charlie named your horse."
"No, I did!" Summer laughed.

As headmaster, Emerson needed to address the recent sectarian issues at Fryeburg Academy. Because the school was founded by members of the Congregational denomination, and continued to be under their control, it received most of their endowment from them. Being a private, rather than a public school supported by tax dollars, it was dependent upon tuition and endowments.

However, it was time to recognize that students and their families were also members of the New Church, the Unitarian Church and dare he say no church? He wished to submit a proposal to the Trustees that would assure that all students, regardless of denominational beliefs, be offered the highest order of instruction.[1]

The Millers quickly adapted to their new routine. Newly independent Charlie was off to work early each morning and returned each evening for supper. Mahayla devoted mornings to reading her father's medical books, before accompanying him on house calls. Isaac enjoyed instructing his new assistant. With Eleanor Jackson now employed at the office, Lydia had time to visit the Anderson family and to attend Temperance meetings. Summer embraced her hosting responsibilities as the wife of the Headmaster, writing, tutoring ten-year-old Etta Anderson, and visiting Mrs. Anderson at the Poor Farm.

Changes

Although the food at their traditional Miller Thanksgiving was the same, the atmosphere was different. It was no longer the "adults" at one table and the "children" at another. Daniel, Rachel, and Isaac with their spouses still sat together. Now, Harriet Chase, Eleanor Jackson, Elizabeth, Jeremy, and Charlie sat at their own table discussing business matters. Emerson and Summer, seated with Mahayla and Thaddeus, discussed their futures. Emerson spoke with much animation of his plans and challenges at the Academy. Summer briefly mentioned her novel. Thaddeus agreed that he was too old to be traipsing around the world, and was looking forward to settling down in an office. Mahayla shared her excitement and concerns about her new studies and ventures. Life was changing for the Millers!

Christmas was depressing for Mahayla and Lydia. Mrs. Jackson and Elizabeth invited Jeremy, Harriet, and Charlie for Christmas dinner.

The original plan was for the rest of them to celebrate Christmas with Emerson and Summer, who was so excited to be hosting her first Christmas dinner! Unfortunately, two weeks before. she became quite ill with nausea, vomiting and exhaustion. The Miller women gave each other knowing glances.

Peter and Rachel decided to visit his sister and family in Brownfield.

Lydia then invited Daniel and Emily for Christmas dinner. Unfortunately, Emily came down with influenza.

That left just the three of them. As Mahayla was setting the table, Mr. Bradley pulled up, explaining his father-in-law was experiencing chest pains and shortness of breath.

"You stay here with your mother," Isaac instructed. "If I need your assistance, I will send Mr. Bradley for you." He grabbed his two bags, hitched the horse to his carriage and was gone for the afternoon.

Mother and daughter were silently eating when Lydia asked, "Have you started packing?"

"Aunt Rachel gave me two old trunks last week and I am all packed."

"How are you ever going to manage handling two trunks?"

"Thaddeus will take me to the train station to ship the trunks tomorrow. They will be waiting for me when I arrive at the college. I am not a child, mother."

After finishing their meal in silence, Mahayla washed the dishes and went into her father's office to study.

Merry Christmas!

---❋---

The big day finally arrived! Mahayla said goodbye to Summer and Emerson the night before. The rest of the family arrived in time to escort her to the train station and wave goodbye. Jonathan came galloping up the road calling, "Dr. Miller! Becky's father collapsed in the barn, and he isn't breathing!"

"Eli!" Rachel cried as Isaac ran to his office to grab his bags. The siblings and their spouses hurried to River View Farm leaving Charlie and Thaddeus.

"I will take you to the train station," Thaddeus volunteered as he placed her two leather suitcases into the carriage.

"Mr. Pierce!" a young man ran up to the carriage. "You have an important telegram!"

Thaddeus' face paled as he read the message from a colleague in Vienna. "I must go to the telegraph office immediately."

"Go ahead, Cousin Thaddeus. I will take her." Charlie threw Charlie Doll in the seat and assisted his sister into the carriage.

"Charlie, have Papa telegraph me about Uncle Eli," she said tearfully.

"I will telegraph you. I know the way to the telegraph office. I'm not stupid."

"No. You're the best brother I could ever have."

"Everybody knows that!"

They arrived just as the train was pulling into the station. Charlie handed the suitcases to a porter and Charlie Doll to his sister.

"For me? I couldn't!"

"I don't need Charlie Doll, but you do. He will make you feel better when you miss me." He walked her to the train.

"Oh Charlie!" she threw her arms around his neck.

"All aboard! All aboard!" the conductor announced.

Mahayla slowly boarded and took a window seat. Charlie stood there waving and grinning, as Mahayla and Charlie Doll waved back.

Thaddeus was panting when he arrived at Dr. Lamson's telegraph office. "I need to send a telegram to Warsaw, Poland."

POGROMS HAVE BEGUN STOP COME TO AMERICA NOW

Historic Characters

Fryeburg Residents:

Dr. D.L. Lamson – Began his medical practice in Fryeburg in 1857. He was indeed a man of many interests! He operated the Western Union telegraph office from his home, took responsibility for the care of the new clock in the steeple of the Congregational Church, was involved in the Fryeburg Water Company, invented a means to light Main Street at night, and was an active member of the New Church.

Alonzo Lewis – Born and raised in Fryeburg, Mr. Lewis was a man of many interests and talents – a businessman, an author, traveler, lecturer, teacher, a trustee of Fryeburg Academy, and active member of the New Church. You will learn more of Mr. Lewis in Book VII.

Reverend Javan K. Mason – Served as pastor of the Congregational Church for nine years after Reverend Stone left to establish The New Church.

Robert Peary – World-renowned Artic Explorer, lived in Fryeburg from 1877-1879 with his mother in a rented house. Upon his graduation from Bowdoin, he did not have any job prospects in his chosen field. He supported himself through a taxidermy business while he made a map of Fryeburg. The Fryeburg Historical Society has two of his stuffed owls and a copy of his map. The Admiral Peary House still stands today as a charming Bed and Breakfast, and you will find Peary Park on Maine Street.

Asa Pike – The grandson of Asa Pike, former owner of the Oxford House, he purchased the Oxford House in 1875, enlarged and modernized it. He also built an addition where the Superior Court of Oxford County and the New Church met.

John Smith – "Uncle Johnny" was a well-known stage driver and innkeeper on Main Street. He sold a portion of his property to the town to build Smith Street which was a direct route from the train station to Main Street.

Ivory Snow – A veteran of the Civil War, served in the 17th Regiment of Maine.

Reverend Baman Stone – Reverend Stone arrived in Fryeburg to serve as the pastor of the Congregational Church. After studying the beliefs of Emanuel Swedenborg, and much soul-searching, he decided to resign his post, rather than cause division within the church. He founded the Church of the New Jerusalem, which originally met at the Oxford House before buying the property on Oxford Street. The church is still active today.

Ann Walker Tarbox – She and her husband owned the first house in Fryeburg to have an indoor bathroom. The house with the original bathtub still stands today on Main Street and continues to be a private resident.

Dr. William Towle – Son of Dr. Ira Towle, he was born in 1830 and raised in Fryeburg. After graduating from Fryeburg, Academy, he traveled out west to mine for gold in the 1850's. Upon his return to Fryeburg, he studied medicine under his father's tutelage. During the Civil War, he served as a surgeon with the 12th and 23rd regiments of Maine. He spent the rest of his life in Fryeburg practicing medicine, serving in a variety of civic organizations, and as an active member of the New Jerusalem Church.

Inventors:

George Corliss–American inventor and manufacturer of the Corliss steam engine. His engine provided the power at the 1876 Centennial Exhibition in Philadelphia.

Charles Hire – American pharmacist, and an early promoter of commercially prepared root beer. His company manufactured and distributed Hires Root Beer. a dry mixture in boxes and sold it directly to consumers and proprietors of soda fountains. They needed to mix in water, sugar, and yeast. His root beer was for sale at the 1876 U.S. Centennial Exposition in Philadelphia

Isaac Singer – American inventor, actor, and businessman, did not invent the sewing machine. He made important improvements in its design and was the founder of Singer Sewing Machine Company, one of the first American multi-national businesses. Originally, sewing machines had been industrial machines, made for garments, shoes, bridles and for tailors. In 1856, smaller machines began to be marketed for home use. However, few were sold because they were too expensive. Singer invested heavily in mass production. By utilizing the concept of interchangeable parts, he was able to cut the price in half, and increase his profit margin.

James W. Tufts- Boston-based manufacturer, Tufts did not invent the soda fountain, but patented a soda fountain called the Arctic Soda Apparatus. His manufacturing company sold more soda fountains than all his competitors combined.

Stephen Whitman–He originally founded a "confectionery and fruit shoppe" in 1842 on the Philadelphia waterfront. He did not invent chocolate confections, but began packaging them in boxes, making it easier to ship to retailers throughout the country. Whitman chocolates are still popular today.

Politicians:
Ulysses S. Grant – A general in the American Civil War, politician, and the 18th president of the United States, who served two terms from 1869 to 1877.
Rutherford B. Hays–An officer in the Civil War, and politician from the state of Ohio. A Republican, Hayes served as the 19th president of the United States from 1877 to 1881.
Samuel Tilden–An American politician who served as the 25th governor of New York and was the Democratic nominee in the disputed 1876 United States presidential election.

Medical Field:
Dr. Elizabeth Blackwell–The first woman physician in the United States. After graduating from Geneva College with a degree in medicine, she was forced to pursue her medical residency in Europe, for there were no opportunities for her in this country. She and her sister, Emily founded New York Infirmary for Women and Children in 1857.
Dr. Emily Blackwell–Elizabeth's younger sister, was the second woman to earn a medical degree at what is now Case Western Reserve University, and pursued further studies in Edinburgh, Scotland, In 1857, Emily and Elizabeth established the New York Infirmary for Indigent Women and Children. Also Emily raised $50,000 to start a medical school in 1859, and in 1860 the infirmary began to train women as assistant physicians.

Dr. Joseph Lister – British surgeon, medical scientist, experimental pathologist and a pioneer of antiseptic surgery, who studied Louis Pasteur's then-novel germ theory. Lister's work led to a reduction in post-operative infections and made surgery safer for patients, leading to him being distinguished as the "father of modern surgery".

Louis Pasteur- French chemist, pharmacist, and microbiologist, famous for his discoveries of the principles of vaccination, and pasteurization. He is also regarded as one of the fathers of germ theory of diseases, His many experiments showed that diseases could be prevented by killing or stopping germs.

Theologians/ Philosophers:

Charles Darwin–British naturalist and author of *The Origin of Species* whose scientific theory of evolution by natural selection became the foundation of modern evolutionary studies.

Ralph Waldo Emerson–an American essayist, lecturer, philosopher, abolitionist, and poet who led the Transcendentalist movement of the mid-19th century.

Karl Marx–German-born philosopher, political theorist, historian, and the author of *The Communist Manifesto*. His ideas and theories collectively known as Marxism have exerted enormous influence on modern intellectual, economic, and political history.

Rev. Ezra Ripley – Minister of the First Parish in Concord, Massachusetts for almost 63 years, his theological views slowly evolved, and he eventually rejected the doctrine of the Trinity. Because of this Unitarian Controversy, a group of parishioners petitioned to leave the church and formed an orthodox congregation in 1825.

Emanuel Swedenborg–Swedish Christian theologian, scientist, philosopher, and mystic. Swedenborg had a prolific career as an inventor and scientist. In 1741, after having mystical experiences, he authored numerous theological books and articles. His followers, called Swedenborgians, started new churches.

Authors:
Anna Sewell–English novelist, is known as the author of the 1877 novel *Black Beauty*.

Mark Twain–"Mark Twain", the pen name of Samuel Langhorne Clemens, is one of the best -known 19th century American novelist, humorist, and essayist. *The Adventures of Tom Sawyer* and The *Adventures of Huckleberry Finn* are classics.

Jules Verne– French novelist, poet, and playwright is best known for his novels *Twenty Thousand Leagues Under the Seas*, and *Around the World in Eighty Days*.

Johann David Wyss–Swiss author, best remembered for his book *The Swiss Family Robinson*.

Fryeburg Landmarks

Fryeburg Academy

Founded in 1792, Fryeburg Academy is one of the oldest private schools in the United States, serving a diverse population of local and boarding students from around the country and the world. 1913 photo of Fryeburg Academy built in brick after the wooden structure burned to the ground in 1851. *Photo courtesy of Fryeburg Historical Society.*

Fryeburg Landmarks

Village School House

This stone building served as the Village School House for many decades. Today it serves as the Fryeburg Public Library *Photo courtesy of the Fryeburg Historical Society*

First Congregational Church of Fryeburg

In 1775 Reverend Fessenden answered the call to pastor the church in a meeting house located in Center Fryeburg. In 1795 a second meeting house was built in the Village to accommodate the growing population and served until 1850. A new church building on Main Street was dedicated in 1850, and still serves as a house of worship today. Reverend Baman Stone served as pastor before leaving to start the Church of the New Jerusalem. *Photo courtesy of the Fryeburg Historical Society.*

The Judah Dana House

This home was built in 1816 by Senator Judah Dana on the corner of Main and River Streets. When it was torn down in 1956 to build the Fryeburg Post office, they discovered a granite lined tunnel that went under the street. According to oral tradition, this home was part of the underground railroad.

This is the location and description of the fictional Senator Benjamin Miller Home which Isaac Miller inherited. *Photo courtesy of the Fryeburg Historical Society.*

The Oxford House

It has been part of Fryeburg since James and Abigail Osgood rented out rooms in their Main Street home in the late 1700's. Over the decades, the property expanded several times until it burned in 1887. An undated photo taken before 1887 *courtesy of the Fryeburg Historical Society*

The Fryeburg Poor House

In April of 1864 the town authorized a committee "The Overseer of the Poor" to purchase a farm, stock, furniture, and all necessary equipment for said farm and to engage an overseer. The farm was disbanded in 1956. *Courtesy of the Fryeburg Historical Society*

The Church of the New Jerusalem

The former pastor of the First Congregational Church of Fryeburg, Reverend Stone left his pulpit to follow his new beliefs based on the teaching of Emanuel Swedenborg. It originally met upstairs in the Oxford House before buying a church building in town.

Discussion Questions and Activities

There are four separate historical concepts presented in *The Life and Times of a Country Doctor*: **medicine, literature, inventions, and philosophies.**

1. To further study the history of American medicine I recommend *Twelve People Who Changed History Through Medicine: A Homeschool Study Guide* published by the Remick Country Doctor Museum & Farm in 2017 which I compiled. Available only on Amazon. All you need is this study guide and a library card for a year's education in history and medicine for middle school and high school students.

2. The second area is literature. Please refer to Author/Literature section. Again, all you need is a library card and the internet. Students can research the lives of the authors and write book reports on the novels of their choosing.

3. The post-Civil War era was a time of new inventions. You can further study the inventions that were exhibited at the 1876 Centennial Exhibition. How did they impact the lives of everyday people? The railroad made an impact in Fryeburg and the entire nation. Describe life before and after the railroad in a town.

The Fryeburg Chronicles Book VI

4. Finally, this was an era of new ideas. What were the original ideas of Karl Marx and/or Charles Darwin? What were the immediate impacts on society? Were they immediately accepted? What are the long-term implications today? I recommend reading chapters 1-5 of *7Men Who Rule the World from the Grave* by Dave Breese.

Who was Ralph Waldo Emerson? What is transcendentalism? Do people today still believe his teachings? Who was Emanuel Swedenborg? Do Swedenborgian churches still exist today?

Many schools' history textbooks go from the Civil War to Teddy Roosevelt, glossing over the many important ideas and accomplishments during this often-over-looked period in our history. Homeschoolers have the freedom to explore the topics in which they are interested to the extent which they prefer.

The Fryeburg Chronicles
Own the Entire Series

Book I *The Amazing Grace* (1781-1784)

Meet the fictional Miller family, early settlers of Fryeburg, Maine as they use their Yankee ingenuity to survive the challenges of rural farm life during the Revolutionary War

Points of Interest:

American Revolution	Herbal Medicine
Architecture	Period Clothing
Basket Weaving	Period Furniture
Cooking on a Hearth	Recipes
Dyeing Wool	Spinning
Farming	Timber Framing
Geometry	Weaving

The Fryeburg Chronicles Book VI

Book II *A Secret and a Promise* (1792-1806)

Now in their 20's, the Miller brothers are beginning new careers, marrying, and having families in a new nation. Attorney Benjamin Miller becomes the first preceptor of Fryeburg Academy.

Points of Interest:

Constitutional Convention
Founding of Washington D.C.
Louisiana Purchase
New Monetary System
Shays Rebellion
Building a Birch Bark Canoe
Building a Cider Press

Cabinet Making
Making Paints
Sewing Quilts
Making Soap
Recipes
Rug Hooking
Williamsburg, VA

Book III *Portraits of Change* (1819-1828)

The Miller family continues with their involvement in the Underground Railroad. Senator Benjamin Miller moves to Washington, D.C. to represent the new state of Maine.

Points of Interest:

Whale Oil Lamps
Noah Webster
Maine Statehood
Missouri Compromise
The Election of 1824
The Underground Railroad

Panic of 1819
Washington Irving
The Erie Canal
Herbal Remedies
Washington, D.C.

The Fryeburg Chronicles Book VI

Book IV *Journeys From Home* (1848-1853)

The nation and the Miller family become more divided. Benjamin's granddaughter leaves Fryeburg to work in a textile mill. A grandson, who is a newspaper reporter, brings home an Irish orphan and some new ideas.

Points of Interest:

The Irish Potato Famine	St. Patrick
The Rise of Textile Mills	1849 Gold Rush
The Free-Soil Party	Moby Dick
The Communist Manifesto	Karl Marx
The Last of the Mohicans	James Fenimore Cooper

Book V *After the Battle* (1860-1867)
Two grandsons, a great-grandson, and family friend of the late Senator Benjamin Miller join the Union forces. Their lives are changed forever at the Battle of Gettysburg. One man loses his life, another his leg. One loses his freedom, and another his soul. Gettysburg is over. The real battle has begun!

Points of Interest:

The Election of 1860
Battle of Bull Run
Civil War Medicine
Andersonville Prison
The hardships and courage of the civilians of Gettysburg

Outbreak of the Civil War
Sharpshooters
Camp Letterman
U.S Christian Commission

Endnotes

Chapter I Scarlett Fever

1. www.microsoftstart.msn.com/en-us/health/ask-professionals/in-expert-answers-on-scarletfever/in-scarletfever
2. www.bing.com/search?q=signs+and+symptoms+of+rheumatic+fever

Chapter II Apoplexy

1. www.cambridge.org/core/books/abs/cambridge-world-history-of-human-disease/apoplexy-and-stroke/8212D32C4D95EBE9F2D748C72B The term apoplexy was used in the 19th century for stroke.

Chapter III A Busy Sunday

1. www.womenshistory.org/education-resources/biographies/elizabeth-blackwell

Chapter IV The Amputation

1. www.famousscientists.org/joseph-lister/
2. www.webmd.com/a-zguides/definition-amputation

Chapter V Mr. Bennett

1. Today the street is River Street.

Chapter VI Tetanus

1. www.thought.com/thehistory-of-the-thermometer
2. www.mayoclinic.org/diseases-conditions/tetanus/symptoms-causes/syc-20351625
3. John Stuart Barrow, <u>Fryeburg an Historical Sketch</u> (Fryeburg, Maine: Pequawket Press, 1938) p 179

Chapter XXII Vienna, Austria

1. Paul Kengor PhD, The<u> Devil and Karl Marx</u> (Gastonia, NC: TAN Books, 2006) p 8
2. Ibid
3. Kengor, p 67-92
4. Kengor, p 63-67
5. Kengor, p 68
6. Kengor, p 79
7. Kengor, p 69
8. Kengor, p 3-4
9. Kengor, p 5
10. Ibid

Endnotes

Chapter XIV Cousin Thaddeus

1. Linda P. Gross and Theresa R. Snyder, <u>Philadelphia's 1876 Centennial Exhibition</u> (Chicago: Arcadia Publishing, 2005) p 8

Chapter XV 1876 Centennial Exhibition

1. Linda P. Gross, p 18
2. Linda P. Gross, p 21
3. Linda P. Gross, p 9
4. Linda P. Gross, p 23
5. Linda P. Gross, p 29
6. Linda P. Gross, p 24
7. www.thoughtco.com/hstory-of-rootbeer-1992386
8. Linda P. Gross, p 40
9. Linda P. Gross, p 44
10. Linda P. Gross, p 47
11. Linda P. Gross, p 55
12. Linda P. Gross, p 67-68, 70
13. Linda P. Gross, p 82
14. Linda P. Gross, p
15. Linda P. Gross, p 71
16. Linda P. Gross, p 16
17. Linda P. Gross, p 112
18. Linda P. Gross, p 126
19. www.cogreatwomen.org/project/martha-maxwell/
20. Linda P. Gross, p 87
21. Linda P. Gross, p 89

The Fryeburg Chronicles Book VI

Chapter XVI The Autumn of '76

1. Henry F. Graff, Editor, <u>The Presidents: A Reference History</u> (New York, Simon & Schuster, MacMillan, 1997) p 261
2. Ibid
3. Henry F. Graff, Editor p 262
4. www.thought.com/thehistory-of-the-thermometer
www.mayoclinic.org/diseases-conditions/tetanus/symptoms-causes/syc-20351625

Chapter XVII Hero of the Ice Harvest

1. Today the street is Elm St.
2. Henry F. Graff, Editor, p 262
3. www.historyisnowmagazine/thestoryoficebeforehomefreezers/theiceharvest

Chapter XVIII The New Church

1. Ola-Mae Wheaton, Margaret W. Briggs, <u>A New Church on Earth A New Church in Fryeburg</u> (Damariscotta, Maine, Victoria Print Shop, 1980) p xi
2. Ola-Mae Wheaton, Margaret W. Briggs p xi, 30
3. Ola-Mae Wheaton, Margaret W. Briggs p 27
4. Swedenborg.com/Emanuel/-swedenborg/theology
5. Ola-Mae Wheaton, Margaret W. Briggs, p 27-28
6. Ola-Mae Wheaton, Margaret W. Briggs, p 3
7. www.uua.org/ Unitarian Universalist Tradition: A Short History

8. history.uconn.edu/wp-content/uploads/sites/36/2014/11/ Gross_Doctor_Ripleys_Church "Doctor Ripley's Church"
9. Swedenborg.com/Emanuel/-swedenborg/theology

Chapter XIX Beginnings and Endings

1. Mark H. Zanger, <u>The American History Cookbook</u> (Westport, Ct. Greenwood Press, 2003) p 199

Chapter XX Mr. Peary

1. Today it is Elm St.
2. This house on Elm Street is now the Admiral Peary House, Bed and Breakfast.
3. John Edward Weems, <u>Peary, the Explorer and the Man</u> (Los Angelos, 1988) p 39
4. Ibid
5. The Fryeburg Historical Society has his two owls on display in their museum, The Samuel Osgood House on 83 Portland St. Fryeburg, Maine.
6. The Fryeburg Historical Society has a copy of his map on display at the Samuel Osgood House.
7. John Stuart Barrows, <u>Fryeburg A Historical Sketch</u> (Fryeburg, ME, Pequawket Press, 1938) p 227
8. John Stuart Barrows, p 178
9. Article by Helen Pike Walker written in 1959 on file at the Fryeburg Historical Society's Research Library located in the Samuel Osgood House.
10. Today it is Peary Park on Main Street in Fryeburg
11. www.difference-between-true-meridian-vs-magnetic
12. Ibid

13. John Edwards Weems p 41

Chapter XXIII A Wedding and a Tragedy

1. John Stuart Barrows, p 220

Chapter XXIV New York

1. Janice P. Nimura, <u>The Doctors Blackwell: How Two Pioneering Sisters Brought Medicine to Women and Women to Medicine</u> (New York City, W.W. Norton & Company, Inc., 2021) p 76
2. Janice P. Nimura Chapter 6 "Paris", Chapter 8 "London"
3. Janice P. Nimura p 201
4. Janice P. Nimura p 243
5. Janice P. Nimura p 69
6. Janice P. Nimura p 262
7. Janice P. Nimura p 207
8. Janice P. Nimura p 233
9. Janice P. Nimura p 243

Chapter XXV Changes

1. Fryeburg Academy Catalog of 1882, p 14

Bibliography

Barrows, John Stuart. <u>Fryeburg Maine: An Historical Sketch.</u> Fryeburg. Pequawket Press. 1938

Beebe, Richard W. <u>The First 200 Years The History of the First Congregational Church in Fryeburg Maine.</u> Center Conway, NH. Walker's Pond Press. 1975

Fryeburg Academy Catalog of 1882

Graff, Henry F. Editor <u>The Presidents A Reference History.</u> New York. Simon & Schuster. 1997

Gross, Linda P., Snyder Theresa R. <u>Philadelphia's 1876 Centennial Exhibition.</u> Chicago. Arcadia Publishing. 2005.

Kengor, Paul PhD. <u>The Devil and Karl Marx: Communism's long March of Death, Deception and Infiltration.</u> Gastonia, NC. Tan Books. 2020.

Nimura, Janice P. <u>The Doctors Blackwell: How two Pioneering Sisters Brought Medicine to Women and Women to Medicine.</u> New York. W. W. Norton and Company. 2021

Weems, John Edward. <u>Peary, the Explorer and the Man</u> Los Angelos. 1988.

Wheaton, Ola-Mae, Briggs, Margaret W. <u>O Jerusalem: A New Church on Earth A New Church in Fryeburg.</u> Damariscotta, Maine. Victoria Print Shop. 1980

Zanger, Mark H. <u>The American History Cookbook.</u> Westport, Ct. Greenwood Press. 2003

Websites:

www.microsoftstart.msn.com/en-us/health/ask-professionals/in-expert-answers-on-scarletfever/in-scarletfever

www.bing.com/search?q=signs+and+symptoms+of+rheumatic+fever

www.cambridge.org/core/books/abs/cambridge-world-history-of-human-disease/apoplexy-and-stroke/8212D32C-4D95EBE9F2D748C72B The term apoplexy was used in the 19th century for stroke.

www.womenshistory.org/education-resources/biographies/elizabeth-blackwell

www.famousscientists.org/joseph-lister/

www.webmd.com/a-zguides/definition-amputation

www.thought.com/thehistory-of-the-thermometer

www.mayoclinic.org/diseases-conditions/tetanus/symptoms-causes/syc-20351625

www.thought.com/thehistory-of-the-thermometer

www.historyisnowmagazine/thestoryoficebeforehomefreezers/theiceharvest

Bibliography

www.Swedenborg.com/Emanuel/-Swedenborg/theology

www.uua.org/ Unitarian Universalist Tradition: A Short History

history.uconn.edu/wp-content/uploads/sites/36/2014/11/Gross_Doctor_Ripleys_Church "Doctor Ripley's Church"

www.difference-between-true-meridian-vs-magnetic

Milton Keynes UK
Ingram Content Group UK Ltd.
UKHW020121221024
449869UK00010B/379